Yvonne Johnson

The Voices
of African American Women

The Use of Narrative
and Authorial Voice in the Works
of Harriet Jacobs, Zora Neale Hurston,
and Alice Walker

PETER LANG
New York • Washington, D.C./Baltimore • Boston
Bern • Frankfurt am Main • Berlin • Vienna • Paris

Library of Congress Cataloging-in-Publication Data

Johnson, Yvonne.
The voices of African American women: the use of narrative
and authorial voice in the works of Harriet Jacobs,
Zora Neale Hurston, and Alice Walker / Yvonne Johnson.
p. cm. — (American university studies. Series XXIV, American literature; vol. 59)
Includes bibliographical references and index.
1. American prose literature—Afro-American authors—History and criticism.
2. American prose literature—Women authors—History and criticism. 3. Jacobs,
Harriet A. (Harriet Ann), 1813–1897. Incidents in the life of a slave girl. 4. Hurston,
Zora Neale. Their eyes were watching God. 5. Walker, Alice, 1944– . Color purple.
6. Influence (Literary, artistic, etc.). 7. Women and literature—United States. 8. Afro-
American women in literature. 9. Afro-Americans in literature. 10. Point-of-view
(Literature). 11. Authority in literature. 12. Narration (Rhetoric). I. Title. II. Series.
PS153.N5J65   810.9′9287′08996073—dc20   94–31070
ISBN 0-8204-2546-X (hardcover)
ISBN 0-8204-4890-7 (paperback)
ISSN 0895-0512

Die Deutsche Bibliothek-CIP-Einheitsaufnahme

Johnson, Yvonne:
The voices of African American women: the use of narrative and authorial voice in
the works of Harriet Jacobs, Zora Neale Hurston, and Alice Walker/ Yvonne
Johnson. –New York; Washington, D.C./Baltimore; Boston; Bern;
Frankfurt am Main; Berlin; Vienna; Paris: Lang.
(American university studies. Ser. 24, American literature; Vol. 59)
ISBN 0-8204-2546-X (hardcover)
ISBN 0-8204-4890-7 (paperback)
NE: American university studies/24

The paper in this book meets the guidelines for permanence and durability
of the Committee on Production Guidelines for Book Longevity
of the Council of Library Resources.

Printed in the United States of America.

Contents

Introduction

The voices of African American women are among the most powerful literary voices to emerge in the latter part of the twentieth century. African American women are recreating and recording a facet of American history that has been neglected and ignored for several centuries. Eighteenth and nineteenth century literary precursors such as Phillis Wheatley, Jarena Lee, Harriet Jacobs and Frances Ellen Watkins Harper have provided literary models for twentieth century African American female authors. The work of such precursors together with the literary accomplishments of early twentieth century African American women has firmly established a literary tradition, and the work of analyzing and illuminating that tradition has begun.[1] Any comprehensive analysis of this literary canon must include an examination of the various rhetorical strategies used by African American women. An explication of the rhetoric of African American women's narratives will necessarily reveal the author's existing cultural milieu as well as the potential of her narrative strategies to influence social-political attitudes.[2]

The literary tradition of African American women differs markedly from that of both white and African American men. The literary texts of males communicate a sense of competition with their literary predecessors. According to Harold Bloom, the Western literary tradition contains "a history of anxiety" in which poets deliberately misread or misinterpret their precursors (30). Bloom's model suggests that such poets are influenced by single precursors.[3] Mary Helen Washington supports the notion of single precursors as she specifically addresses the male African American literary tradition. Washington states:

every anthology of *the* Afro-American literary tradition has set forth
a model of literary paternity in which each male author vies with his
predecessor for greater authenticity, greater control over *his* voice,
thus fulfilling the mission his *forefathers* left unfinished (Darkened 33).

Unlike this model of competition with a single precursor, the
African American woman writer willingly embraces multiple
predecessors.

Alice Walker has formally acknowledged Zora Neale Hurston
as her literary "foremother," and has stated that were she condemned to a desert island for life she would "unhesitatingly"
choose to take Hurston's *Their Eyes Were Watching God* with
her (*In Search* 86). In addition to Hurston, however, Walker
also acknowledges other precursors such as Rebecca Jackson,
Phillis Wheatley, and Ida B. Wells-Barnett, one of the first African American feminists in this country. The willingness to
recognize and validate such "foremothers" distinguishes the
voices of modern African American female writers. Maggie
Humm concludes that if the African American woman's literary voice has been "supported by a past nurturing female community, in contemporary life Black feminist critics also prefer
a common Black voice in literature to the (male) notion of
single precursors" (110). Writers such as Alice Walker, Toni
Cade Bambara and Toni Morrison most certainly draw from a
broad literary and historical tradition.

The African American female writer, while embracing her
predecessors, does modify and revise previous texts. According to Henry Louis Gates Jr., the practice of revising, troping,
or "signifyin(g)" upon literary predecessors is a firmly established practice within the African American canon (xxii). The
African American woman's voice, a voice that has been repressed and oppressed by racism and sexism, has been pre-
served in oral traditions that have been recounted from one
generation to another. Joanne M. Braxton states: "By passing
along cherished recipes to subsequent generations, by testifyin',
by telling the story of their religious conversions, or by singing the spirituals or the blues, Black women helped to revise
and extend this oral tradition" (*Wild* xxii). Virginia Woolf, referring to the legacy of literature, reminds her readers that
"masterpieces are not single and solitary births; they are the
outcome of many years of thinking in common, of thinking by

the body of the people, so that the experience of the mass is behind the single voice" (68). The voices of African American women simultaneously represent and revise the thinking and experiences of many generations.

The purpose of this book is to examine the narrative strategies, with particular emphasis on the authorial and narrative voices, of three texts written by African American women. Although most of the narratives written by these women will be referenced, the three principal texts under consideration are *Incidents in the Life of a Slave Girl* by Harriet Jacobs; *Their Eyes Were Watching God* by Zora Neale Hurston; and, *The Color Purple* by Alice Walker. I chose these three narratives because of their intertextual connections, connections that are often linked to the rhetorical strategies used by the authors. According to Braxton, there are "distinct similarities" between Jacobs's and Hurston's texts, not only because of the presence of an "outraged mother," but also "in the pairings of the narrator-granddaughter with a protective and powerful grandmother" (*Wild* 302). The similarities between Hurston's and Walker's texts are easily identified because Walker has written at length about Hurston's influence upon her.

An examination of the authorial and narrative voices in these three texts, their intratextual as well as intertextual connections, reveals not only revolutionary revisions within a literary tradition, but also the historical development of consciousness and voice among African American women writers. According to Barbara Christian, "The use of history in the novels of contemporary African-American women writers, then, is constant and consistent" (*Wild* 328). Recent writers have certainly had more freedom than their predecessors to include controversial social-political discourse in their narratives and to "revision" their history. I have selected one nineteenth century slave narrative and two twentieth century novels in order to trace the development of voice in African American women since 1861, to place it in historical context, and to offer an explanation for the emergence of a powerful African American women's voice in the latter part of the twentieth century.

An explanation of the structure of each of the three narratives is an important part of identifying the authorial and narrative voices of each text. By focusing on the relationship between the author, the "implied author," the narrator, and the reader, I have not only identified the voices within the text, but also more effectively interpreted what they are saying. Just as the author creates an image of herself, either as narrator or implied author, she also creates an image of the reader, and addresses the narrative either implicitly or explicitly to that reader. Her narrative can be considered most successful when the created author and the created reader have the same values and beliefs.[4] According to Gerard Genette, the "voice" of a narrative can be examined only "by ripping apart a tight web of connections among the narrating act, its protagonists, its spatio-temporal determinations, its relationship to the other narrating situations involved in the same narrative, etc." (215). My purpose has been to rip apart the intratextual and intertextual narrative connections in order to locate both the individual and "common" voices within these texts.

The discourse of the created author or narrator, which is directed toward a created reader or narratee, is another aspect of voice. The examination of voice within the structure of a given narrative necessitates, to some extent, an explication of the culture of the implied reader. The "voices" within these texts, therefore, must be accounted for not only from the perspective of the narratives themselves, but from the cultures that helped create them.

For the purposes of this analysis, I have decided to dissociate to some extent the definition of the term "voice" from the traditional "point of view" focus. Tzvetan Todorov distinguishes between voice as "the presence of the speech-act as a whole in the discourse," and perspective which is "the point of view from which we observe the object." Todorov does, however, consider the two "inextricably linked" (28). Speech-act theory takes into account not only the utterances within the text, but what is implied by those utterances.[5] As a speech-act, voice can also be considered an indicator of self-knowledge and is used as such not only by those who write and critique fictional narrative, but also by feminist psychologists such as Nancy Chodorow, Carol Gilligan, and Mary Field Belenky and others.[6] In commenting on the works of Chodorow, Gilligan, and Belenky, Elizabeth A. Flynn states: "All three books suggest that women and men have different conceptions of self and different modes of interaction with others as a result of their different experiences, especially their early relationship with the mother" (425). Knowledge of the self, then, is particularly linked to the concept of "voice" in women. Since the three texts under consideration are narrated by women, voice as an indicator of self-knowledge is evident in the various narrative enunciations. The term "voice," therefore, is used not only in reference to narrative voice, to "point of view," but to the process of bringing the self to consciousness, the process of becoming a speaking subject.

In his book *The Signifying Monkey*, Gates reads Hurston's *Their Eyes Were Watching God* "in such a way as to move from the broadest notion of *what* it thematizes through an ever-tighter spiral of *how* it thematizes; that is, its rhetorical strategies" (181). Gates admirably demonstrates the process of revision and troping that connects *Their Eyes Were Watching God* to Walker's *The Color Purple*. While I also point out connections between Hurston's and Walker's texts, my analysis moves in the opposite direction from *The Signifying Monkey*. While Gates moves from interpretation *toward* narrative structure, my analysis moves *from* narrative structure toward interpretation. I believe that the process of moving *from* rhetorical analysis as a hermeneutic theory can be used to identify the convergence of voice with its historical context. This process is necessarily "deductive" as Roland Barthes prescribes in his essay, "Introduction to the Structural Analysis of Narratives," and therefore moves from a model of narrative analysis to an interpretation of what is being said (253).

In *Inspiriting Influences*, Michael Awkward analyzes the intertextuality of four novels written by African American female writers. These novels include *Their Eyes Were Watching God* and Walker's *The Color Purple*. While his analysis also includes an examination of the structure of each of these novels, his purpose is to establish that

> the textual affinities between black women's works generally exist not simply as the result of a common sexual and racial oppression, but, rather, most frequently occur as a function of black women writers' conscious acts of refiguration and revision of the earlier canonical texts (Awkward 4).

Awkward's purpose is to reveal how African American women writers *denigrate*, or "blacken" their texts by infusing "Black cultural 'spirit' into Western 'matter'" (10). While I agree that African American female writers consciously refigure and re-vise earlier texts, I conclude that it is difficult, if not impos-sible, to separate the textual affinities of these novels from the sexual and racial oppression that inspired them. The discur-sive elements, or voices, of these texts form a necessary part of the structure of each narrative; moreover, the narrative loses meaning if the speaking subject is separated from her discourse. One may conclude, then, that an explication of both the struc-ture and discourse of these narratives is necessary to establish the speaking subject.

The role the narrator plays in the narrative as well as the "states of speech" employed by that narrator, whether they are narratized, transposed into indirect style, or mimetic, are as-pects that determine narrative voice (Genette 171). Although these features of narrative discourse are important to a textual analysis, the most important element is the point of view of the narrator, and her relationship to the author and/or per-son addressed, for "it is necessary to assume the existence be-tween this 'person' and his language of a straight descriptive relation which makes the author a full subject and the narra-tive the instrumental expression of that fullness" (Barthes 283). Wayne Booth calls this person the "implied author," an "ideal, literary, created version of the real man; he is the sum of his own choices" (*Rhetoric* 74). The interrelationship between the author, implied author, narrator and protagonist that is re-vealed in the discourse of the texts under consideration, in addition to other commentaries by the authors, enable the reader to understand the dialogue within each narrative as well as the intertextuality of the three narratives.

Each of these narratives is written with an audience in mind. Just as the author is, more or less, connected to her narrator, the individual addressed by that narrator is, more or less, con-nected to the actual reader. The addressee, or narratee, of Jacobs's *Incidents in the Life of a Slave Girl* approximates what the author hopes will be an actual reader. Harriet Jacobs for-mally addresses her narrative to the white women of the North. On the other hand, the narratee of Walker's *The Color Purple*, addressed as "Dear God," would not usually be thought of as an actual reader.

In his study *Narratology: The Form and Function of Narrative*, Gerald Prince determines that "the portrait of a narratee emerges above all from the narrative addressed to him" (12). In both *Incidents in the Life of a Slave Girl* and *The Color Purple* a portrait of the narratee becomes visible. In *The Color Purple*, Walker's protagonist, Celie, actually describes her narratee. She tells Shug that God is "big and old and tall and graybearded and white. He wear white robes and go barefooted" (201). Perhaps because, in this instance, the narratee is quite unlikely to respond to this narrative, and because the narrator, Celie, very desperately needs a response, an element of unreality is added by her prayer-letters. According to Wayne Booth, the most successful narratives are those in which the "created selves, author and reader, can find complete agreement" (*Rhetoric* 138). Actually, there are often as many as four created images in a narrative; the implied author, the narrator, the narratee, and the implied reader. These created images produce the authorial and narrative voices.

The narratives I have analyzed are all women-centered. The narrators, implied authors and narratees are, with one exception, unquestionably gender specific. Jacobs's narratees are female since her narrative is addressed primarily to Northern white women. Hurston's narratee is also female but is an African American woman who lives in the community of Eatonville. Walker's narratee, while initially introduced as a patriarchal image, is later revised, or "(re)visioned", as an androgynous spirit or being.

Both narrators and narratees are either female or androgynous in the primary works under consideration. The narrators are women who attempt "to close the gaps between the narratee, the addressee, and the receiver" (Warhol 29). The narrators of these texts use various "engaging" strategies to build connections between the created universe of the text and the "real" world of the reader. One of my purposes is to explore the characteristics and possibilities of feminist narrative strategies. According to Susan S. Lanser, "A feminist narratology might acknowledge the existence of multiple texts, each constructed by a (potential) rhetorical circumstance" ("Toward" 355). The authorial and narrative voices of these texts, weave a web of connectedness that not only brings the various plots within each text into rhetorical interaction, but provides an intertextual connection as well. Both Jacobs and Hurston use rhetorical strategies that can be described as subversive. Jacobs's *Incidents in the Life of a Slave Girl* is written in the mode of the nineteenth century domestic novel and as such it conforms to the prescribed conventions. The voice that emerges from the narrative, however, does not represent that era's "cult of true womanhood." According to Barbara Welter, the "true woman" judged herself and was judged by her peers according to her adherence to "four cardinal virtues—piety, purity, submissiveness, and domesticity" (Welter 96). Without these virtues a woman was nothing, but with them she was promised happiness and power. While Jacobs seemingly embraces this point of view, she actually subverts it by arguing that slave women, like white men, should be judged on complex moral grounds (Yellin, "Introduction" xxxi).

Hurston's *Their Eyes Were Watching God*, like Jacobs's narrative, is written as a romance; however, according to bell hooks, "the focus on romance is a device Hurston uses to engage readers while subtly interjecting a subversive narrative" (hooks, "Zora" 6). This subversive narrative with its multiple plots contains a voice that "appears to address everyone even though it speaks in its deepest structure to a select few" (hooks, "Zora" 8). Hurston's narrative is designed to have widespread appeal, especially in the white community, but like Jacobs's the voice that emerges from this "romance" is revolutionary. The goal of Hurston's protagonist, Janie, is freedom, but unlike Harriet Jacobs, Janie seeks her freedom within the African American community and within heterosexual relationships that have repressed her consciousness of herself.

The merging of the authorial and narrative voices into a search for a centered consciousness makes Hurston's *Their Eyes Were Watching God* a powerful expression of African American voice. Hurston's protagonist, Janie, "speaks" herself into existence, prompting Gates to refer to *Their Eyes Were Watching God* as a "speakerly text" (170). Karla Holloway suggests that Hurston's texts are connected by a "lyric narrative voice," a voice that becomes strong enough to "speak itself" into existence (36). Hurston did not originate this voice but was influenced by at least two "foremothers"—Frances Ellen Watkins Harper, and more importantly, Harriet Jacobs.[7]

While Hurston's protagonist, Janie, *speaks* herself into existence, Walker's Celie *writes* herself into existence in letters that are never meant to be read. "In this epistolary novel, the narrator of Celie's tale is identical to the author of Celie's letters" (Gates 248). Genette considers the form of narration to be most delicate when, as in Walker's *The Color Purple*, "the journal form loosens up to result in a sort of monologue after the event."[8] Thus, at the time of reading, Celie is the heroine and already someone else. While Celie is the protagonist imaged within the narrative, she is simultaneously the author who has retrospectively penned her own narrative.

Walker does not present "true" discourse in *The Color Purple*, for this novel is recounted in Celie's letters. "But, through Celie's mode of apparently reporting speech, underscored dramatically by her written dialect voice of narration, we logically assume that we are being shown discourse, when all along we never actually are" (Gates 24). Through the increasing self-awareness and sophisticated "dialogue" of these letters, the reader becomes aware of Celie's desire for self-knowledge.

Like the protagonists in *Incidents in the Life of a Slave Girl* and *Their Eyes Were Watching God*, Celie's goal is freedom, and like Janie, Celie's freedom is to come through self-knowledge. While Janie seeks her self-knowledge and empowerment within heterosexual relationships, Celie finds hers in a relationship with Shug, the woman who becomes her sister, friend, and lover. Walker revises Hurston's text by enlarging the possibilities for emotional and sexual relationships. Barbara Christian states: "In a sense, Walker in *The Color Purple* does for the sexual relationships between black women what Hurston in *Their Eyes Were Watching God* did for sexual relationships between black women and men" (184). While the voice that emerges from Walker's *The Color Purple* is more powerful and much less restricted by social convention than those of its predecessors, it shares some common goals.

The narrative and authorial voices of these three narratives share a common tradition, a tradition that is specifically female as well as African American. The development of this female African American tradition has resulted in the empowerment of the voices under consideration. Virginia Woolf predicted that a door would open for women and there would take place "the most interesting, exciting and important conversation that has ever been heard."[9] African American voices in the latter part of the twentieth century are addressing all women; in a real sense they are addressing all of humanity by calling on people to bridge the communication chasms that separate them. According to Barbara Christian, "women of color can no longer be perceived as marginal to the empowerment of all American women" and an "understanding of their reality and imagination is essential to the process of change that the entire society must undergo in order to transform itself" (185).

African American women are "(re)structuring" and "(re)-visioning" their history, a history that has often been ignored by both mainstream and feminist scholarship. Patricia Hill Collins points out that "feminist theory has also suppressed Black women's ideas" by assuming that white, middle-class values and ideas are "universally" applicable to women as a group (7). Collins identifies a distinct "Afrocentric women's culture" which allows the African American woman an "outsider-within" stance. The outsider-within "functions to create a new angle of vision on the process of suppression," a stance which aids in the reclamation of the history of African American women (11). The perspective of African American female scholars coupled with newly or rediscovered historical documents and fictional narratives will allow scholars to revise and revision the lives and voices of an important, but long-neglected, portion of American history. As Barbara Christian stated in an interview with me, there is a tremendous need to bring fictional narrative and historical documents together in order to recover what has been lost to these women.

Chapter One

Harriet Jacobs's
Incidents in the Life of a Slave Girl

Incidents in the Life of a Slave Girl (1861) is, according to Joanne Braxton, "the only known full-length work by an Afra-American [sic] writing about her experiences as a slave woman" (*Black* 23). Of over one hundred thirty existing slave narratives, only sixteen were written by women, and most of those women were free northerners (Fox-Genovese *Plantation* 461). Although *Incidents* was first published in Boston in 1861, it was for many years overlooked as an important slave narrative. In the early twentieth century it was categorized as a false slave narrative, a work of fiction written by the white abolitionist, Lydia Maria Child. This important work remained almost forgotten by the general public until the Civil Rights Movement of the 1960s, and then the Women's Movement of the 1970s created new interest in it. Jean Fagan Yellin, literary historian, biographer, and editor of the most recent publication of *Incidents*, became convinced that the narrative was not fiction, but a historically verifiable document. She proceeded to research newly available documents, notably those in the Post Archive at the University of Rochester. In 1981, she succeeded in establishing the veracity of the narrative (Yellin, Introduction xiii-xxv). From that date the narrative has been reexamined from both literary and historical perspectives. The following analysis will examine three areas in which the voice of the author/protagonist manifests itself: the voice of the narrator herself; the audience to whom it is addressed, the narratee(s) and implied readers; and finally, the narrative perspective or point of view.

The narrator and the author are the same in autobiographical texts, but in Jacobs's narrative the author distances herself by creating a fictional narrator, Linda Brent. Because of the distancing between author and narrator, Harriet Jacobs's name will be used when referring to the author, but her pseudonym, Linda Brent will be used in reference to the narrator and protagonist.

According to Susan Sniader Lanser, every written text has a "voice that 'speaks' and another, usually silent consciousness that 'hears'" (*Narrative* 114). While the voice "speaks" through the narrator, the consciousness that "hears," the audience to whom the text is addressed, is often referred to as the narratee. The authorial voice of *Incidents* certainly speaks through the narrator, Linda Brent, but can also be examined as a separate entity. Lanser suggests that this authorial voice speaks "through the text's title, through whatever information is provided about the text's genre, purpose, and mode and through the author's name" (*Narrative* 124). The reader of *Incidents in the Life of a Slave Girl* is made aware by the title that the text is a slave narrative; by the subtitle, *Written by Herself*, that it was written by the author rather than an amanuensis; and, that the author is an African American woman who presumably managed to escape from slavery. The title tells the reader that the author and the narrator speak with the same voice, that the author/narrator is the person "who speaks" and "who sees" through the text. The title also indicates that the text is not a comprehensive autobiography but rather a series of events from a life.

The title page contains other relevant information. The author's name tells the reader that she is a woman. The reader may have presumed the author's gender from the title, but her name serves as confirmation. Lanser considers the "*noted* presence" of a woman's name on the title page a sign that the narrative voice is female "in the absence of markings to the contrary" (*Narrative Act* 167). Although Jacobs equates herself with her narrator in the preface, her explicit statement is not necessary because readers automatically link the narrative and authorial voices in an autobiographical context.

The reader may correctly infer that the relation of events from Jacobs's life is designed to elucidate certain aspects of slavery. In her preface Jacobs addresses her narrative to a specific audience and states her reasons for concealing her real name. She informs her reader that she has concealed place names and "given persons fictitious names" because she "deemed it kind and considerate towards others to pursue this course" (1). Jacobs undoubtedly wished to protect members of her family who were still living in slavery, but the reasons she gives for concealing places and names may cause current readers to question her motives further. Readers may try to discern other reasons for this concealment through the process of what Mary Louise Pratt terms *implicature*.[1] The authors of most male slave narratives did not conceal their names; however, it was very common for nineteenth century women to write under the auspices of a *nom de plume*. "During the eighteenth and nineteenth centuries, anonymous publication was considered, especially in England, to be the only decorous alternative for women" (Lanser, *Narrative Act* 127). Current readers may also correctly conclude that the topics addressed by the narrator of *Incidents* were proper grounds for authorial concealment. Jacobs recounts her master's numerous attempts to either seduce or coerce her sexually. Even though her identity is partially concealed, narrative conventions would not allow her to reveal specifics about Dr. Flint's attempts to rape her. She tells the reader that a young slave girl in her position "will become prematurely knowing in evil things," and that Dr. Flint swore to kill her "if I was not as silent as the grave" (28). Jacobs knew these were topics that might not be welcomed by her audience, but that a semi-anonymous narrative would allow her to at least broach the subject of sexual coercion.

In addition to the preface, the original publication of *Incidents* also had an introduction written by its editor, Lydia Maria Child.[2] While introductions by white abolitionists were common in slave narratives, the purpose of this introduction is twofold. The usual reason for such an introduction was to attest to the veracity of slave narratives, to "endorse" the narrative in such a way as to make it more appealing to the readership at which it was most often aimed. Child is certainly attesting to the veracity of Jacobs's narrative, but she is also preparing the audience for the rather controversial and perhaps shocking revelations that are to follow.[3]

Although Harriet Jacobs's narrative has been historically verified, her fictionalized narrator, Linda Brent, is what Lanser calls a "public narrator" because she addresses an idealized reader who represents the public (*Narrative Act* 138). Both Jacobs in her Preface and Brent in the body of her text address white women of the North in the hope that they will be able to identify with her plight, that they will perhaps recognize a shared bondage, and that they will be moved to aid their sisters who are chattel slaves. Shared gender between narrator and audience is a central part of the narrative's desired effect: identification and empathy. Lanser states:

> Identity includes such aspects of social status as profession, gender, nationality, marital situation, sexual preference, education, race, and socioeconomic class. Of all these categories, gender is the most universally central to *linguistic* activity in Western culture, because Indo-European languages are notably marked for gender distinctions. Gender is also central to *cultural* communication because of the importance gender distinctions play in everyday life. Sex differences therefore permeate the uses of language and condition the reception of discourse (*Narrative Act* 166).

Gender identity between narrator and narratee, or audience, encourages direct contact between the two and leads to what Lanser calls "narrative self-consciousness" (*Narrative Act* 87). In the case of *Incidents* this self-consciousness may be predicated on the assumption that women would more readily listen to the life experiences of another woman than men. William L. Andrews states specifically that slave women like Harriet Jacobs "needed a sense of an empathetic female audience, not an interrogating male one, before they could write or speak freely" about their experiences (*Tell* 247).

Narrator-narratee communication or "I-you" contact creates an opportunity for the narrator of *Incidents* to reveal awareness of the communicative process in which she is involved. The narrator may actually communicate a large range of attitutes toward the narratee and toward the narrative process itself (Lanser, *Narrative Act* 178). Brent assumes that her reader is aware of many of the abuses that slaves endured. She uses phrases such as "the reader probably knows" and "we all know" to indicate knowledge and perhaps understanding that both narrator and reader share. Brent seems to be asking for such understanding when she queries: "Reader, did you ever hate?" (40). On the other hand, she obviously worries about the reader's response to her confession of what was considered sexual misconduct when she queries, "What *could* I do?" (53).

And finally, she exhibits the anger and frustration she feels as she rebukes the thoughtlessness of her northern readers. She states: "Surely, if you credited one half the truths that are told you concerning the helpless millions suffering in this cruel bondage, you at the north would not help to tighten the yoke" (28). Although her attitude toward her narratee ranges from confident to worried and angry, Jacobs's narrator always preserves a degree of formality. This formality keeps a "friendly but respectful" distance between the narrator and her audience, a distance that is mandated by her gender, her race, and her position in society.

Robyn R. Warhol has identified what she considers gendered methods of communication by narrators. She distinguishes between feminine "engaging" and masculine "distancing" strategies used by nineteenth century narrators and argues quite convincingly that these strategies can be identified as "gendered interventions": "The interventions that I see as being most clearly gendered are those in which the narrator establishes his or her attitude toward the reader, toward the characters, and toward the act of narration itself" (20).

Engaging narrators attempt to bring together the 'you' addressed directly in the text, the reader implied by that direct address, and the actual reader of the text.[4] The narrator of *Incidents* uses engaging interventions by addressing the 'reader' or 'you' in a manner designed to evoke recognition and identification in the actual reader, a reader that is not likely to resemble Linda Brent in the least. Brent directly addresses her narratee on the subject of slavery: "O, you happy free women, contrast *your* New Year's day with that of the poor bondwoman!" (16). Brent then describes the lot of the slave mother who "sits on her cold cabin floor, watching the children who may all be torn from her the next morning; and often does she wish that she and they might die before the day dawns" (16). By direct address and direct comparison, she pulls her reader into the text and into empathy with the plight of slave mothers.

An engaging narrator does not usually name specific narratees but does "use names that refer to large classes of potential actual readers" (Warhol 33). Jacobs's narrator often calls on large groups of potential readers. Indeed, the passages in which she addresses those readers seem designed to evoke the most empathy and understanding. For example, the narrator informs the reader that she "made a headlong plunge," meaning that she took a lover, possibly in order to thwart Dr. Flint's advances toward her. She immediately follows this confession with a direct address: "Pity me, and pardon me, O virtuous reader! You never knew what it is to be a slave" (55). Again, in addressing a specific audience, she says: "But, O, ye happy women, whose purity has been sheltered from childhood . . . do not judge the poor desolate slave girl too severely!" (54). It is worth noting that while Brent engages the reader by direct address, she also distances herself somewhat by pleading for "a poor desolate slave girl" in the third person. Her purpose as narrator/protagonist is to deflect harsh judgement and retain her empathetic audience.

Warhol describes an engaging narrator as one who frequently addresses the narratee and who encourages the reader to identify as much as possible with the situation presented in the narrative (34). Jacobs's narrator addresses the narratee as 'you' in at least nine passages of her narrative. She also addresses the narratee directly as 'Reader' in at least five passages. Almost all of these passages direct the reader's attention and sympathy not only to her personal situation but also to the plight of those still in bondage. She states: "Reader, it is not to awaken sympathy for myself that I am telling you truthfully what I suffered in slavery. I do it to kindle a flame of compassion in your hearts for my sisters who are still in bondage, suffering as I once suffered" (29). In another passage designed to emphasize common knowledge between narrator, narratee and reader, she states: "We all know that the memory of a faithful slave does not avail much to save her children from the auction block" (6). The "we" in this passage is particularly aimed at women, but the narrator also includes northern men as her addressees in one passage. She asks: "In view of these things, why are ye silent, ye free men and women of the north?" (29). The narrator's direct appeals to "you" and "Reader" are interspersed among those narratees more specifically named. These more general designations serve to broaden the scope of her appeal because they can signify any actual reader; however, whether they are more specific or more general, they serve to engage the reader.

While distancing narrators often "inscribe the addressee as a potentially 'bad reader,'" the engaging narrator assumes that her readers are in sympathy with her (Warhol 36). This assumption allows Jacobs's narrator to discuss sexual matters with her reader that far exceeded those contained in "polite" nineteenth century discourse. Perhaps because of the delicate nature of her subject, the narrator seems compelled to overjustify her situation, and in her overjustification she reveals something of the culture she is addressing.[5] The overjustification of Jacobs's narrator reveals narratees who are not 'bad readers' but possibly limited sympathizers. An example of this limited sympathy is revealed in Brent's opening statement of the chapter in which she describes her seven year confinement. She says, "I hardly expect that the reader will credit me . . . but it is a fact" (148). One of the explicit purposes of this narrator is revealed in her attempt to convert her readers to her point of view.

The engaging strategies of Jacobs's Brent are most noticeable when one compares them to the *Narrative of the Life of Frederick Douglass*. Frederick Douglass, like Jacobs, is writing to an audience in the North. Both he and Jacobs are addressing readers who they hope will be able to aid their cause, but Douglass might be considered a distancing rather than an engaging narrator. Not once in his narrative does he address "you" or "the reader." Although his object is undoubtedly to win a sympathetic readership, the effect of the narrative strategy is to make Douglass more of an object than a subject, to make the narrative almost appear to be written so many years after the event that the author was able to remove himself from the emotional content.[6]

When his master gives him to the slavebreaker, Mr. Covey, Douglass reports that it was only a few months before "the dark night of slavery closed in upon me; and behold a man transformed into a brute!" (*Narrative* 75). Not only does Douglass present himself as an object, a brute, but he also distances himself from his pain: "My sufferings on this plantation seem now like a dream rather than a stern reality" (*Narrative* 75). As Douglass removes the emotional content of his sufferings, as he distances himself from his past, he also distances himself from his readers.

While the narratee or addressee of *Incidents* is the consciousness that "hears" and is the consciousness directly addressed,
the author is also writing to a "consciousness" that is just be-
neath the surface of the text. Brent never directly addresses
this consciousness; however, her editor states in the Introduction that she hopes "every *man* [emphasis mine] who reads
this narrative" will never send a fugitive slave back into bondage (4). The narrator is keenly aware of this cultural consciousness, for the autobiographical structure itself has traditionally
been a male domain. Not only has it been a male domain, but
the form of autobiography that was developed during the Renaissance made it a white European male domain. Sidonie
Smith considers autobiography "a convention of patriarchal
culture" that causes women to be "doubly estranged" when
they write about themselves. "Since autobiography is a public
expression, she speaks before and to 'man'" (49).

As an African American slave woman, Jacobs's relationship
to the autobiographical contract is even more complex. She is
forced to address her white women readers through a cultural
convention in which she had no part, the "cult of true womanhood." Mid-nineteenth century women's magazines, such as
The Ladies' Repository, Godey's Lady's Book, The Ladies' Garland,
and *The Ladies' Companion*, characterize the "true woman" as
gentle, innocent, pure, pious, domestic, submissive, and somewhat helpless. The stories and sermons of this period stress
the duties of obedient, submissive wives and mothers. According to Linda M. Perkins, "This 'true womanhood' model was
designed for the upper and middle-class white woman, although
poorer white women could aspire to this status" (18). A slave
woman living in the antebellum South, however, had no hope
of acquiring or maintaining the virtues demanded of the "true
woman." Although Jacobs is exempted from the myth of the
lady, or "true woman," she makes use of this cultural construct
to reach her audience.

Brent is simultaneously asking for understanding and perhaps acceptance from her audience while challenging the attributes of "true womanhood." Purity was considered the most
important characteristic of a "true woman." Jacobs admits that
she is not sexually pure, but asks her reader to consider both
her immediate circumstances and the circumstances of all

women held in bondage. She describes the character of her master, Dr. Flint, whom she terms a "vile monster," and she characterizes his attempted seduction of her as "the war of my life" (19). According to Angela Davis, "The sexual contest was one of many arenas in which the black woman had to prove herself as a warrior against oppression" (14). Undoubtedly, Jacobs was such a warrior; one method she uses to resist her owner is by taking a white lover. She attempts to place a man of her own choosing between herself and Dr. Flint in the hope that her action might help her gain freedom or at least a kinder master for herself and her children. She appeals to her readers: "I feel that the slave woman ought not to be judged by the same standard as others" (56). These "others" were her white female readers who were bound by images of "true womanhood." Although this appeal would seem to support the "cult of true womanhood," further examination of her text reveals that neither slave nor free women actually live up to the standards of the cult.

Nineteenth century women's magazines often portray women who prefer death to loss of purity. If women who lost their purity did not die, they usually went insane. Ella Harwood, the protagonist of a serial story in *The Ladies' Garland*, gives her heart too hastily to Alfred Lyston. When she learns that he is betrothed to another, "her mind was swung from its moorings" (84). According to Barbara Welter, "The frequency with which derangement follows loss of virtue suggests the exquisite sensibility of woman, and the possibility that, in the women's magazines at least, her intellect was geared to her hymen, not her brain" (100). Ella Harwood's story, entitled "The Blighted One," does not end with a simple derangement. Ella takes her own life by throwing herself in the river. "Yes, the lovely Ella Harwood had found a watery grave. Like the beauteous Sappho of other days, she had sung her last song to her unfaithful lover, and the trembling wave closed over her fairy form!" (84). Using a common euphemism of the day Jacobs states that Dr. Flint "threatened me with death and worse than death," but it is obvious from the narrative that Brent never contemplated either death or insanity because of her lack of purity (32). Brent chose to engage her master in verbal warfare, using both the oral and written language to reject his power over her. "*Inci-*

dents entered the field of women's literature and history transforming and transcending the central paradigm of death versus virtue" (Carby 59). In this instance, Jacobs actually rejects
the euphemism of death versus loss of purity and replaces it
with "Death is better than slavery" (62).

While Brent gives "lip service" to the cult of true womanhood, she questions its validity for either slave or white women.
Southern white women were expected to be pure, but Jacobs
notes that "Southern women often marry a man knowing that
he is the father of many little slaves" (36). According to Jacobs,
the institution of slavery "deadens the moral sense" of the pure
southern lady. She implies that many southern ladies are dishonorable for ignoring their husband's transgressions and men-
tions two "ladies" who exhorted their husbands to free their
slave children as "honorable exceptions" (36). The reader is
implicitly asked to compare the helpless slave woman to the
"dishonorable" southern lady. Jacobs also informs her readers
that southern white women are often victims of both patriarchy and slavery. Although southern white women may "have
romantic notions of a sunny clime," they are inevitably destined to be disappointed for the "husband in whose hands she
has placed her happiness pays no regard to his marriage vows"
(36). Thus, jealousy, hatred, and dishonor are a part of the
southern slaveowner's home. Jacobs exposes the myth of the
white woman's purity. Purity and innocence are not a reality
for either slave or free white southern women.[7]

Not only is Brent not driven insane or to suicide by her loss
of virtue, she fails to fulfill another important characteristic
of a "true woman." The second characteristic of a "true woman"
was submissiveness. "Submission was perhaps the most feminine virtue expected of women. Women were the passive, submissive respondents. The order of dialogue was, of course,
fixed in Heaven" (Welter 102). Jacobs effectively uses dialogue
in her narrative to subvert, among other things, the tradition
of submission. According to Andrews, "There is more dialogue
in *Incidents* than in any other black autobiography of the antebellum era" (*Tell* 277). This dialogue reveals a powerful narra-
tor/protagonist who resists the efforts of her master to dominate her. At one point, after repeated threats and insults, Brent
states: "'You have struck me for answering you honestly. How I

despise you!'" To her disbelieving master she then thunders: "'You have tried to kill me, and I wish you had; but you have no right to do as you like with me'" (39). The dialogue of Jacobs's white benefactress, Mrs. Bruce, also reveals a lack of submissiveness. Mrs. Bruce's male relative scolds her for harboring a fugitive slave and violating the law. Mrs. Bruce replies that she is well aware of the law and its penalties. She states:

> "Shame on my country that it *is* so! I am ready to incur the penalty. I will go to the state's prison, rather than have any poor victim torn from *my* house, to be carried back to slavery" (194).

Neither Linda Brent nor Mrs. Bruce are passive, submissive respondents. Both women, one a slave, the other a white upper class woman, use dialogue to assert their independence. Such dialogue subverts the image of the "true woman."

The third characteristic that women were expected to exhibit was domesticity. The "true woman" was admonished to retire from "the busy highways of ambition;" she was to "wander in the shady, green lanes of domestic life." Her duties were unquestionably at home where "unseen, unfelt she extends her influence far and wide" (C.F.D. 245). Through the role as wife and mother, the role designed for her by Almighty God, woman was destined to influence the world.

Domesticity was a constant theme in mid-nineteenth century women's magazines. Southern white women did not fit into this view of domesticity for it reflected the northern view of separate spheres and production outside the home. The domestic life of southern women on plantations was inextricably bound within the slave system, a system that was involved in labor and production (Fox-Genovese, *Plantation* 78-79). Slave women did not fit into this theme either, for they were overtly chattel, without benefit of legal marriage. Even when they were able to obtain their freedom, this white, middle-class image was generally denied them. When her narrative ends, Brent does not have a home of her own. She states: "The dream of my life is not yet realized. I do not sit with my children in a home of my own. I still long for a hearth stone of my own, however humble" (201). The narrator does not wish for marriage and domesticity, but she obviously expresses a sincere wish for a haven for herself and her children.

The fourth characteristic of a true woman was piety. Nineteenth century literature, especially women's magazines, portrayed women as just a little lower than the angels, certainly closer to Heaven than mere men. According to *The Ladies' Repository* of 1843, "In no part of society does Christianity exert a more benign influence than over woman" (H.G. 7). The women's magazines disparaged the thought of an impious woman. "It is not contempt with which we contemplate the spectacle of a woman who has so forgotten her sex and her nature as to proclaim herself an unbeliever—it is horror!" (C.F.D. 112). Brent's spirituality does not reflect that of the cult of true womanhood. Although Brent despises the hypocritical Christianity practiced by slaveholders, and her voice also rejects what she calls "religion," her spirituality offered "a strong moral code in the midst of an immoral system" (Carby 57). Jacobs's moral code as well as her seeming acquiescence to the "cult of true womanhood" encouraged the white woman reader to identify with her.

Incidents is written in the mode of the nineteenth century domestic novel and as such it conforms to the prescribed conventions. While Jacobs overtly rejects the Christianity as practiced by slaveholders, and actually seems to embrace at least the ideal of domesticity, she subverts the notions of purity and submissiveness embodied within the cult of true womanhood in two ways. She presents herself as a moral person in the midst of an immoral system. Even though she is a slave woman—a woman with a primitive nature in the eyes of her readers—she assures her readers of her desire for virtue. In the face of Dr. Flint's assaults she tells her readers: "I had resolved that I would be virtuous, though I was a slave" (56). She also tells Dr. Flint of her desire to preserve her virtue because of the love she has for another man. She tells Dr. Flint that the man she loves "never insulted me," and she assures her master that, "he would not love me if he did not believe me to be a virtuous woman" (39). Jacobs also undercuts the belief in "true womanhood" by demonstrating throughout her narrative that neither black slave women nor white free women are able, or often even willing, to meet *all* the requirements and demands of the cult. Actually, the result is a confused picture of identity and behavior on the part of both white and slave women. Slavery—and on a deeper level, patriarchy—is presented as the ultimate cause for such a confused and distorted portrait of southern society.

Jacobs expands her narrative by incorporating forms of discourse that go beyond the narrator-reader relationship.She does this by dialogizing her narrative, by allowing her characters to speak for themselves through reconstructed dialogue. By giving her characters "voice" she is also able to use African American dialect in a very persuasive manner and to reveal the heteroglossia of which all discourse is composed. Although this is one reason her narrative was considered a fictive work, this deliberate "fictionalization" of her autobiography actually gives it power and is one more method of subverting the cultural limitations placed upon slave narrators. According to Andrews, slave narrators broke with literary convention in the 1850s. Douglass, in *My Bondage and My Freedom*, and Jacobs, in *Incidents in the Life of a Slave Girl*, were among the first narrators to use dialogue and dialect to lend authenticity to their narratives ("Novelization" 24). Unlike Douglass, Jacobs uses dialogue to address the power of patriarchy as well as the institution of slavery. Andrews states: "By dialogizing her narrative exposé of `the patriarchal institution,' Jacobs illustrated graphically the discursive nature of male-female power relationships" (Andrews, *Tell* 270). Dialogue, therefore, communicates Jacobs's message most powerfully to her audience.[8]

While Jacobs writes within the conventions of the "cult of true womanhood," the voice that emerges from the narrative sends a number of messages to its readers. The narrator tries to anticipate her readers' objections and to persuade her readers of her earnestness, sincerity, and honesty throughout the narrative. Jacobs's voice is, on the surface, the voice of an outraged mother and woman calling on her Northern white sisters to come to her assistance, but like many African American voices it is also reflective of what W.E.B. DuBois termed "double-consciousness." DuBois states: "Such a double life, with double thoughts, double duties, and double social classes, must give rise to double words and double ideals, and tempt the mind to pretence or to revolt, to hypocrisy or to radicalism" (146). Jacobs's voice not only reflects the double-consciousness caused by racial oppression, but the narrator of *Incidents* allows a number of voices to infiltrate the text. The multiple voices that speak through the text—devoted daughter and grand-daughter, runaway slave, outraged mother—reflect the gender of the narrator.

Jacobs speaks for women, both slave and free, who have no rights to their bodies. She subverts the stereotypes of the black whore and the white lady by demonstrating that the "cult of true womanhood" was truly a myth. This subversion of the myth, however, also reveals a double-consciousness, a conscious-ness that is simultaneously bound to and alienated from the very women Jacobs is addressing. Lanser agrees with Wayne Booth's statement that "We are constituted in polyphony," but she also argues that polyphony "is more pronounced and more consequential in women's narratives" ("Toward" 350). While the dialogization of voice discussed earlier reveals multiple voices, the polyphonous voice of *Incidents* can perhaps best be revealed by examining the narratees—the audience directly addressed in the text, and the implied readers—the audience that is inferred by the text.

Incidents reveals a narrative voice designed to please white audiences, a voice that is asking for aid from its readers, and its values are designed to appeal to the "delicate ears" of its readers. According to Elizabeth Fox-Genovese, the "deep struc-ture" of the text argues that slave women, like white men, should be judged on complex moral grounds. White women of the nineteenth century wrote within their gender, "but the writ-ings of Afro-American women have departed significantly from this model" ("Statue" 73). Perhaps this moral identification with males arises from the fact that slave women like Jacobs "suffered the pain of childbirth and the sorrow of losing chil-dren and had labored like men" ("Statue" 74). Jacobs's identi-fication with white men rather than white women in this in-stance simply demonstrates that "neither masculinity nor femininity exists as an absolute" ("Statue" 73). In arguing that the slave woman "ought not to be judged by the same standard as others," Jacobs employed the rationale used by white males (56). In this instance her gender identification was not related to her sexuality. She states that her goals are simply freedom and a home for her children, goals that a nineteenth century audience could accept, but it can be argued that she had less obvious goals, goals that are implied by her narrative's relationship to its audience.[9]

Narratees, implied and actual readers are extremely important to the narration of *Incidents*. The narrator wishes to communicate effectively with her audience; she can do so only by engaging the sympathies of that audience. Roman Jakobson's diagram of a speech act proposes that narrative emphasizes either its relation to context or its relation to receiver.[10] "Speech act theory recognizes the importance to successful communication of the speaker's social and psychological identity, of his or her roles, relationship to the audience, and attitude toward the message" (Lanser, *Narrative Act* 83). Jacobs's narrative undoubtedly emphasizes its relation to the receiver, in this case, white women who might be able to identify with her plight and who might be in a position to aid other women such as she. The text that emerges is clearly "a code through which the narrator and reader are signified throughout the story itself," a communication that indicates "a world situated with respect to narrator and reader" (Culler 195). Brent assures the reader of her sincerity and the veracity of her narrative: "Reader, I draw no imaginary pictures of southern homes. I am telling you the plain truth" (35). The twentieth century reader early realizes that, as Smith puts it, "Jacobs's readers were accustomed to a certain degree of propriety and circumlocution in fiction" (37). By directly addressing her reader in this way, Jacobs not only "established that hers was the voice of a representative black female slave but she also made an appeal to the "sisterhood of all women" (Carby 50).

Jacobs appeals to the sisterhood of all women by presenting herself as a woman who shares some of the same values and trials as her readers, and who is, moreover, engaged in a heroic effort to overcome almost insuperable obstacles. She is undoubtedly aware of the risk she takes by making her private life public, but she hopes to enlist the sympathy of her readers by enabling them to see through her eyes throughout the duration of her narrative. Wayne Booth, in describing Emma Bovary, states: "the isolated heroine can do for herself what no other narrator could possibly do for her. Very little heightening of her character is needed to make us unite with her against the hostile world around her" (*Rhetoric* 276). This is certainly the view that the reader has of Harriet Jacobs. Two scenes in *Incidents* particularly portray the heroine as an isolated individual pitted against a hostile world. In the first, Brent is hidden by friends in Snaky Swamp while the town of Edenton, North Carolina is being turned inside out in search of her person. She relates a dreadful night alone in the swamp. "I passed a wretched night; for the heat of the swamp, the mosquitos, and the constant terror of snakes, had brought on a burning fever" (113). The second scene is the nine by seven foot garret that housed Brent for almost seven years.[11] Brent was hidden by her grandmother in the space between the roof and ceiling of a shed attached to her grandmother's house. During her seven years of confinement she had no contact with her children and could view them only through a small hole she bored in the wall of her den. She says, "O, those long, gloomy days, with no object for my eye to rest upon, and no thoughts to occupy my mind, except the dreary past and the uncertain future! I was thankful when there came a day sufficiently mild for me to wrap myself up and sit at the loophole to watch the passers by" (116). By presenting herself as an isolated heroine, then, and through her appeals for empathy, Jacobs hoped to win the support of her audience.

Brent's images of an isolated heroine linked her to her audience. The narrator appears as a helpless woman who is dependent upon friends and family for support. The audience to whom this narrative is addressed could empathize with the image of a mother who is separated from her children, a woman whose life is warped, whose physical and spiritual being is deformed by her chatteldom. Brent engages her reader with one other image connected to her confinement. She confides that she passes her time, not only by reading her Bible, but also by sewing clothing for her children. The devoted mother as seamstress is another image with which her audience was familiar. According to *Godey's Lady's Book*, all women, "be of what earthly rank they may, however gifted with intellect or genius, or endowed with much beauty—have always some little handiwork ready to fill the tiny gap of every vacant moment" (305). These images, connected to confinement and domesticity, serve to heighten the empathy that Jacobs seeks to establish with her audience.

The links between Jacobs and her reader(s) are her narratees.[12] Jacobs's principle narratees were women in the North whose point of reference was the "cult of true womanhood." The narrator was undoubtedly aware of the value judgements of her readers and approached the topic of sexual relationships with trepidation. Katherine Fishburn states that both southern ladies and women slaves were held in bondage: while the "lady was deprived of her sexuality, the black woman was identified with hers" (11). The white woman was put on a pedestal while the "less civilized" black woman was often despised and perhaps envied for her sexual "freedom." Jacobs mediates this misconception of women who are treated as no more than chattel and who are subject to sexual abuse by directly addressing her narratee. She states: "Pity me, and pardon me, O virtuous reader! You never knew what it is to be a slave; to be entirely unprotected by law or custom; entirely subject to the will of another" (55). She realizes that much of her subject matter may be offensive to her readers, for she states: "This peculiar phase of slavery has generally been kept veiled; but the public ought to be made acquainted with its monstrous features, and I willingly take the responsibility for presenting them with the veil withdrawn" (2). According to Diane Roberts, "Jacobs argues for a new dispensation for black women, a more flexible definition of what a good woman might be" (139). Jacobs asks for more than mere toleration and sympathy, she asks for a new definition of the true woman.

Actually, the narrator never totally withdraws the veil in *Incidents*. She does, however, tell the reader more of her situation than her mere statements reveal. "Narrative always says less than it knows, but it often makes known more than it says" (Genette 198). Twentieth century readers can gain insight into this aspect of nineteenth century America by examining the silences, or ellipses, found in the text. Brent states that her master, in seeking to seduce her, peopled my young mind with unclean images, such as only a vile monster could think of" (27). True to nineteenth century narrative, however, she does not tell the reader exactly what these images were.[13] Jacobs obviously had a sexual relationship with the lawyer she calls Mr. Sand, but she withholds the details of this relationship. She states, however, that her decision to take a lover was motivated by the desire to have at least some control over that portion of her life. "There is something akin to freedom in having a lover who has no control over you, except that which he gains by kindness and attachment" (54). The slave woman was not only subject to all the labor and punishments of male slaves but also often denied any freedom in sexual matters. Minrose Gwin says of her decision: "Brent's gesture of taking a white lover is, in this sense, a grand show of choice, as she herself emphasizes" (58).

Brent's decision to take a lover is certainly in tension with her identification with the values of true womanhood. It is not, however, in tension with the voice that undercuts the myth of the cult. In her assertion of the right to choose a lover based on an affectionate relationship, Jacobs's voice once again subverts societal notions of purity and submissiveness for women. Brent never discusses her relationship with the man she calls "Mr. Sand." The reader can only assume from her brief statement that she possibly had strong feelings for him—that they had perhaps a love relationship. When she learns that he is planning to marry another woman, and determines to confront him with the fate of their children, she says only, "Painful memories were so busy within me" (126). According to Genette, "One can tell *more* or tell *less* what one tells" (51). In her account of her relationships with both Dr. Flint and Mr. Sand, there are two important narrative spaces. These narrative spaces not only paint a portrait of one of the narratees but also appeal to the readers' emotions in such a way that the account will be acceptable to Jacobs's nineteenth century female readers. The narrative spaces allow Jacobs to address both nineteenth century notions of purity and the reality of interracial sexual relations without offending the sensibilities of her northern white female readers.

In addition to direct address and gaps in the narrative, questions or what Gerald Prince calls "pseudo-questions," can reveal certain "knowledge and defenses" connected to the narratee (14). Brent directly challenges the narratee and the values associated with the "cult of true womanhood" when she asks, "What would *you* be, if you had been born and brought up a slave?" (44). She uses this question to condemn the institution of slavery and to ask her readers' empathy for her situation. Brent is addressing a commonly held prejudice toward slaves—the belief that they were untrustworthy—when she explains how she convinced Dr. Flint that she had escaped to the North while she was really hiding in her grandmother's attic. She asks: "Who can blame slaves for being cunning? They are constantly compelled to resort to it. It is the only weapon of the weak and oppressed against the strength of their tyrants" (100). And, finally, she challenges the belief that Africans were created to be slaves by asking, "And then who *are* Africans? Who can measure the amount of Anglo-Saxon blood coursing in the veins of American slaves?" (44). Jacobs, herself, was of mixed heritage. In her first chapter she states: "In complexion my parents were a light shade of brownish yellow, and were termed mulattoes." She also tells the history of her maternal grandmother, "the daughter of a planter in South Carolina," obviously a white man, who freed his Anglo-African family at his death (5). Jacobs's grandmother and her siblings were dragged back into slavery as they tried to escape North and each were sold to different owners. The question that Jacobs raises, then, is rhetorically directed in regard to the entire population of African Americans and is also one that personally affects her.

Although *Incidents* is addressed primarily to northern white women, another group is addressed near the end of the narrative. In her twenty-third chapter which she entitles "Prejudice Against Color" the narrator, Brent, addresses African American men and women who are servants to whites in the North. Brent encountered what she terms "cruel prejudice" in the North, prejudice that resulted in her transportation in Jim Crow railroad cars and her banishment from a hotel dining room to the kitchen for her supper. After she was refused service in the dining room, Brent took her meals in her room. Although she is informed that the other "colored" servants of boarders were "dissatisfied because all were not treated alike," she states: "I staid [sic] a month after this, and finding I was resolved to stand up for my rights, they concluded to treat me well" (177). Brent ends her chapter by directly addressing African American servants: "Let every colored man and woman do this, and eventually we shall cease to be trampled under foot by our oppressors" (177).

Although African American servants are the only other narratees directly addressed, Brent indirectly addresses at least one other narratee. Wolfgang Iser calls such a narratee an "implied reader."[14] While it can hardly be argued that *Incidents* is written and addressed primarily to Northern white women, in her chapter entitled "Incidents in Philadelphia" Brent seems to be addressing a male audience. During her escape to the North, Jacobs was aided by an African American minister and his wife. She recounts a conversation she had with Mr. Durham, the minister, in which he asks her about her daughter and marriage status. She remembers: "I frankly told him some of the most important events of my life. If he was desirous of being my friend, I thought he ought to know how far I was worthy of it." He, in turn, advised her not to be so open about her past, for her openness "might be met with contempt." Durham reassures her that if she trusts in God and lives according to "good principles, you will not fail to find friends" (161). "This confession scene poses an implicit question for the male reader of *Incidents*: will he be a respectful 'friend,' or merely peruse Jacobs's past with 'idle curiosity,' if not 'contempt'? (Andrews, *Tell* 250). One other dialogue is directed toward the male reader. Brent's uncle, Benjamin, attempts an escape to the North but is captured and brought back to Edenton. Benjamin describes his feelings in a male-directed statement. "When a man is hunted like a wild beast he forgets there is a God, a heaven. He forgets everything in his struggle to get beyond the reach of bloodhounds" (22). The implied reader in both these scenes is male. In the first the reader, male or female, is presented with, and asked to identify with, a woman's perspective. In the second scene a more male perspective is presented.

Finally, Brent indirectly addresses what Andrews calls an "idealized marginal community," an interracial community composed of both white and black women whose common bonds are those of patriarchy and whose common goals are the casting off of those bonds (*Tell* 252). These women might best be represented by Lydia Maria Child and Amy Post, neither of whom are addressed within the narrative, but whose encouragement aided the publication of *Incidents*.[15] The goals and ideals of this women-centered community can be seen by examining the voice of the narrator as it is expressed through the perspective or point of view of this narrative.

An understanding of the voice of the narrator of *Incidents* is incomplete without examining her point of view or narrative perspective. A certain amount of ambiguity surrounds the terms "point of view" and "narrative perspective." Since the purpose of this study is to examine narrative voice, however, the two terms will be used interchangeably and will emphasize the "relationship between narrator and narrated event" (Lanser, *Narrative Act* 17). The narrative construction of *Incidents* is certainly influenced by the writer's interaction with the culture in which she lives. Because the writer and narrator of this text are one and the same, the narrator's voice and the author's sense of self are interwoven throughout the presentation of the text. According to Sidonie Smith, "self-interpretation emerges rhetorically from the autobiographer's engagement with the fictive stories of selfhood," and from "the polyphonic voices of discourse" (49). The discourse presented by Linda Brent/Harriet Jacobs, then reveals her concept of self, how that notion of selfhood is influenced by the culture in which she lived, and finally, how that self expresses itself through the narrative text.

In appropriating the form of the autobiographical slave narrative Harriet Jacobs faced several challenges. As a woman she was using a literary form that, until the eighteenth century, was designed to tell the "public" life of men. Since women were confined to the domestic sphere in the nineteenth century, the ideal woman was characterized by silence, not discourse. What made Jacobs's situation even more complex were the issues of race and class. These issues caused Jacobs to become "doubly or triply the subject of other people's representations" to the effect that several sets of stories are layered into the narrative (S. Smith 50). In order to locate the narrative perspective of *Incidents*, it is necessary to understand the impact of a black female voice upon a literary genre that did not provide a non-patriarchal language with which it could express itself.

John Blassingame, in *The Slave Community*, argues that *Incidents in the Life of a Slave Girl* is not an authentic slave narrative because it lacks the "representativeness" of other slave narratives. He criticizes the story not only because it is too orderly but also because it is "too melodramatic: miscegenation and cruelty, outraged virtue, unrequited love, and planter licentiousness appear on practically every page" (373). Blassingame's analysis is articulate and convincing, but like many historical analyses, it reflects a male perspective.[16] When addressing slaves as a whole, Blassingame invariably uses male constructs; for example, he states: "Although unlettered, unarmed, and outnumbered, slaves fought in various ways to preserve their manhood" (284). In addressing the portrait of the slave that emerges from Southern literature, Blassingame states: "The major slave characters were Sambo, Jack, and Nat" (224). The only chapter in Blassingame's account that is not overwhelmingly male oriented is his chapter entitled "The Slave Family," but even within that chapter, he addresses women as a whole only to state: "Women in most traditional West African societies were subordinate to men" (177). According to Hazel Carby, Blassingame's notion of a representative slave narrative is one that tells "what went on in the minds of *black men*" (Carby 367).

   Historians and literary critics alike have defined the autobiographical genre in androcentric terms. Sidonie Smith examines the literary criteria for "representativeness" in autobiography and concludes: "Clearly, all the model types are male models, a fact that suggests once again the degree to which Western discourse has conflated 'male' norms and 'human,' or universal, norms" (9). The woman who has written autobiography, then, has been forced to appropriate a male tradition and to justify to her reader the appropriation of that tradition while speaking "a fragile heteroglossia of her own, which calls forth charged dramatic exchanges and narrative strategies" (S. Smith 50). *Incidents* may indeed appear to be more melodramatic than male slave narratives, and it certainly deals with sexual harassment and licentiousness in a manner not consistent with those narratives, but its "differentness" does not preclude its validity. The point of view expressed in Jacobs's narrative shares common ground with views expressed in male slave narratives, but the narrative voice that emerges is quite distinct from that in the male slave narratives.

   Despite the fact that slaves were stereotyped as lazy, slave narrators seemingly espouse the work ethic by reiterating the beliefs of many Americans that hard work will be rewarded. Stephen Butterfield says of slave narratives: "On the surface, they are close to the values of white Protestant America" (13). These values are readily apparent in *Incidents* but are in each instance invariably challenged and undercut by Jacobs's coded voice. A large part of this narrative gives at least lip service to the Protestant Work Ethic. According to Fox-Genovese, slave narrators used constructs that Northerners could understand: "the emphasis fell increasingly upon the inherent opposition between slavery and the work ethic, slavery and initiative, slavery and democracy" ("Strategies" 161). Brent describes how her grandmother "by perseverance and unwearied industry," had managed to obtain for herself and the children that remained to her, "a snug little home" (17). Her grandchildren most certainly desire such a home for themselves. "We longed for a home like hers" (17). Jacobs later reveals, on the contrary, that this home was not always a haven secured through hard work, but was substantial enough to arouse jealousy on the part of white patrollers who searched it in the wake of Nat Turner's Rebellion. The patrollers were shocked to discover that Aunt Marthy had a large trunk of linens, and one responded with "'you seem to feel might gran' 'cause you got all them 'ere fixens. White folks oughter have 'em all'" (65). Although the home was spared, the captain in charge of the search patrol "pronounced a malediction on the house" as he left it and said "it ought to be burned to the ground" (66).

The manner in which Linda Brent describes her grandmother's life in the first chapter of *Incidents* is similar to Horatio Alger's approach in his rags-to-riches stories and reflects white society's strong belief in the Protestant work ethic. Aunt Marthy was once a slave, had lost several of her children on the auction block, and had herself been purchased and set free when she was fifty years old. The implication of the narrative is that she had earned what little she had only through perseverance and hard work. The grandmother became the town's baker while still a slave, and was able to keep part of the profits "which was saved for a fund to purchase her children" (6). Despite this overt testimony to the work ethic, Aunt Marthy was to learn a bitter lesson in regard to promises made to slaves. She had learned to bake crackers and had attracted so many requests for this item from the people of Edenton,

North Carolina that her master allowed her to bake at night after the household chores were done. She was allowed to keep what little she earned from her "midnight bakings," and thus accumulated three hundred dollars which she planned to use to buy her children's freedom. Her mistress asked for the money to buy herself some candlesticks and never repaid the loan. "The reader probably knows that no promise or writing given to a slave is legally binding; for, according to Southern laws, a slave, *being* property, can *hold* no property" (6). In this instance, Jacobs's narrator, is challenging both the code of honor as it related to the ruling class and the work ethic that promised commensurate reward for one's labor.[17]

Stephen Butterfield argues that the work ethic is seen as "a partial solution to the problems slavery creates for the slave even if it only advances him (sic) in the system or enables him to buy his way out" (14). Brent's voice, however, challenges the value of the work ethic to buy freedom or security for those enslaved. Although her grandmother works hard, and although Brent herself perseveres, shrewdness and patience, and an awareness of their double-consciousness seems to aid them more than hard work. Aunt Marthy, while presenting a guileless face to the world, hides her granddaughter in her attic, and Brent is willing to be confined for seven long years while she awaits an opportunity to escape.

In addition to challenging the Protestant work ethic, Brent also addresses the role of the church and the hypocrisy of slaveowners. Butterfield states that "Most slave narratives are strongly Christian," and the narratives' authors "praise God, prayer, good works, and the anti-slavery cause" (15). Like other slave narrators, Brent carefully distinguishes between what she believes to be "true" Christianity and the religion practiced by slaveholders. She relates an occasion when she visited a Methodist class meeting that was taught by "the town constable—a man who bought and sold slaves, who whipped his brethren and sisters of the church at the public whipping post, in jail or out of jail. He was ready to perform that Christian office anywhere for fifty cents" (70). Jacobs's point of view resembles, in part, that of Frederick Douglass who loathes the "man who wields the blood-clotted cowskin during the week" and then "meets me as a class leader on Sunday morning" (*Narrative*

121). Frederick Douglass distinguishes between "the pure, peaceable and impartial Christianity of Christ" and the "corrupt, slaveholding, women-whipping, cradle-plundering, partial and hypocritical Christianity of this land" (*Narrative* 120). Both Jacobs and Douglass prefer not to call the religion of the slaveholding South Christianity, but refer to it simply as "religion." This point of view corroborates Sterling Stuckey's study of slave culture. He states: "Religion was for many slaves... an African version of Christianity marked by an awareness of the limits of the religion of whites" (85).

Brent's voice diverges from those of male slave narrators on the subject of religion. The voice that speaks against unchristian practices also addresses an issue that seldom appears in male narratives. Brent, addressing one of the issues that concerned women, reveals that if a minister had a child by a white woman not his wife, he would be dismissed from his position in the church, but "if she is colored, it does not hinder his continuing to be their good shepherd" (74). She also relates how her master, once he had become a communicant in the Episcopal church, urged her to become his mistress by telling her that if she was faithful, she would "`be as virtuous as my wife'" (75). Jacobs's voice is raised against this type of sexual harassment, an issue that simply would not have been addressed by male slave narrators.

Brent does praise those who are "true" Christians. She introduces the reader to an Episcopal clergyman who insisted on preaching to the slaves, and whose wife taught slaves to read and write. Needless to say, he did not stay long in the town of Edenton. She describes an old black man named Fred, "whose piety and childlike trust in God were beautiful to witness" (72). This slave asked Brent to teach him to read and write so that he could learn to read the Bible. Although he was over fifty, Brent marvels at the quickness in which he learned to read the New Testament. In a passage that is similar to an incident in the narrative *The Gift*,[18] in which the protagonist learns to read by a miracle, Uncle Fred tells Linda that he always prays to God "to help me understan' what I spells and what I reads. And he does help me, chile" (73). The humble hearts of the white clergyman and the black slave indicate a shared religious faith that exposes the hypocrisy and mere "religion" of slaveholders. "Worship of God and Christ is a means of ideological struggle against the contemptible Christianity of the slaveholder" (Butterfield 18). Indeed, the simple Christianity and child-like faith of both Linda Brent and her grandmother, Aunt Marthy, serves to assure them that God is on their side and supplies the courage that Brent needs to sustain her in her long confinement and escape to the North.

The one area in which the narrators of slave narratives reveal a departure from "Christian" principles is in their relations with their masters or other white people. Frederick Douglass considered it a "positive virtue" to deceive slaveholders and William and Ellen Craft told of the numerous occasions they lied to and deceived white Southerners with pride and humor (Butterfield 16). Brent is no exception. She entitles one of her chapters "Competition in Cunning" and proceeds to tell the reader how she deceived Dr. Flint through a rather elaborate scheme. She knew that he was constantly searching for her and she determined to convince him that she was indeed in the North. Her Uncle Phillip brought her New York newspapers from which she took street names and addresses, and she wrote two letters which a family friend, a free black who was a sailor, carried to New York and mailed back to Dr. Flint and her grandmother. She tells with pride how Dr. Flint then brought his letter to her grandmother, gave a false account of its contents, and then urged her Uncle Phillip to go in search of her to bring her back to Edenton. The narrator seems to be both amused and angered at his attempt to out-deceive her. She is, however, convinced that she has outwitted him for she states: "The fact that Dr. Flint had written to the mayor of Boston convinced me that he believed my letter to be genuine, and of course that he had no suspicion of my being any where in the vicinity" (132).

Male slave narrators, while recording similar instances of deception, depict confrontations with their masters or other slaveowners in violent terms. Frederick Douglass, in his *Narrative of the Life of Frederick Douglass*, describes a violent confrontation with Mr. Covey, the man who had hired him out as a slave laborer. Once the blows had been struck, Douglass states: "We were at it for nearly two hours" (82). These were blows that enabled Douglass to liberate himself.[19] Jacobs's narrative also contains some liberating blows, but unlike Douglass's, these blows were verbal.

When Dr. Flint, who had been sexually harassing Brent, learned that she was in love with a young freedman, he angrily rebuked her and informed her that she was above the "'insults of such puppies.'" Brent replied in a similar manner and Dr. Flint struck her. Brent immediately exclaims: "'You have struck me for answering you honesty. How I despise you!'" (39). Although the doctor had sheared her hair and struck her in anger on several occasions and had once injured her rather severely by throwing her down a flight of stairs, he never resorted to having her whipped. Jacobs, in turn, never seemed to hesitate in speaking her mind. A factor in Brent's ability to answer Dr. Flint's demands with some amount of freedom may have been her grandmother's presence. Brent describes her grandmother's relationship with Dr. Flint: "Though she had been a slave, Dr. Flint was afraid of her. He dreaded her scorching rebukes" (29). Indeed, after Dr. Flint struck Linda in her grandmother's house, Aunt Marthy ordered him out: "'Get out of my house!' she exclaimed. Both Jacobs and her grandmother used verbal confrontation to protect themselves and their families. Perhaps because slave women lacked the physical ability to confront their owners in any other way, they were forced to rely on their wit and their speaking ability; ultimately, their voices, to assert themselves as human beings. Butterfield states that the slave narrator's identity is linked to his desire for freedom and "the act of resistance is the backbone of his selfhood" (18). Linda's selfhood is tied to her voice, for her act of resistance is expressed in that voice. According to Joanne Braxton, "Women resort to wit, cunning, and verbal warfare as forms of rebellion; in *Incidents in the Life of a Slave Girl,* Linda employs verbal warfare and defensive verbal postures as tools of liberation." This verbal warfare or "sass" as it has been called is of West African derivation and refers to those women accused of witchcraft and thus associated with the trickster God, Sxu, who were forced to drink a poisonous concoction made from the bark of the sass tree. "Whenever Linda under sexual attack, she uses sass as a weapon of self-defense; she returns a portion of the poison the master has offered her" (Braxton, *Black* 32). The narrator's voice assumes special dimension in the account of this slave woman, for it signifies her ability to survive physically as well as mentally.

Brent uses her voice to protect herself against the lustful designs of Dr. Flint, but the reader discovers that she does not have such recourse in dealing with his jealous wife, Mrs. Flint. Although jealousy caused Mrs. Flint to participate in what might be considered a double victimization of her slave, Brent's perspective is somewhat different in regard to her mistress. Brent gives a full account of the wrongs committed against her by both Dr. Flint and his wife, but her resentment seems to be tempered by the knowledge that the two women are victims of the patriarchal system that holds them both in bondage to some degree. Jacobs is undoubtedly illustrating how white women suffer from their husbands' betrayals. Mrs. Flint tried to control her husband's desire for Brent, and when she could not, she revenged herself on the only person possible, her slave. Her jealousy made her perversely cruel, an enraged monster, and Brent gives a full account of her acts. Minrose C. Gwin states:

> In their jealous depravity, these white women become specters of slavery itself. Far from adhering to the code of the cult of True Womanhood, which demanded piety and morality, these white women, as depicted by their female slaves, become evil creatures, nurtured by the institution that allows them and their husbands absolute power over other human beings (61).

Jacobs's narrative certainly indicts those women who wronged Brent, including her first mistress who taught her to read, indicated that she would have her freedom eventually, and then willed her as a slave to her niece. The narrator, however, records mixed feelings. "As a child, I loved my mistress; and, looking back on the happy days I spent with her, I try to think with less bitterness of this act of injustice" (8). Even Mrs. Flint, who made Brent walk through the snow with no shoes on because their squeaking annoyed her, and who threatened her life because she thought her husband was the father of Brent's child, is treated less harshly by the narrator than is probably warranted. Jacobs's discussion of Mrs. Flint is another example of the way in which she undercuts the notion of "true womanhood," for not only does Mrs. Flint fail to conform to the ideal, but both women are portrayed, to some extent, as victims of an evil system. She says, "I pitied Mrs. Flint," no doubt in recognition of the reality that bound both women. Sshe tempers her pity, however, for she distinguishes between those Southern women who do not trouble themselves about the fact that their husband is the "father of many little slaves" and those who try to right what is wrong. She says, "I have myself known two southern wives who exhorted their husbands to free those slaves towards whom they stood in a 'parental relation;' and their request was granted" (36). She further places her mistress's actions "within a history of acts of betrayal toward three generations of women in her family: herself, her mother, and her grandmother. Each served as faithful servant, each trusted to the honor of her mistress, and each was betrayed" (Carby 52). "Jacobs's Brent repeatedly pairs female slaves and slaveholders, but nowhere does she show a slave and a mistress who can sustain affection for each other" (Yellin 91). Gwin characterizes the relationship between mistress and female slave as one of "obverse images" (46). These "obverse images" reveal a narrative perspective that diverges from that perspective generally offered by male slave narrators.

Brent's voice has special significance and force in this slave narrative when it speaks as an outraged mother. Braxton uses the term "outraged mother" to identify the slave mother. "She is a mother because motherhood was virtually unavoidable under slavery; she is outraged because of the intimacy of her oppression" (*Black* 19). The narrators of male slave narratives do not parallel or mirror this voice in any way. It belongs only to women. "Motherhood opens the pathway to greater self-awareness and, like sass, becomes a vehicle for the retrieval of lost self-respect" (Braxton, *Black* 33). Motherhood also seems to provide knowledge of the self and a world view that is absent in the narratives of males. The experience of having and being a mother often gives women a sense of connection with other humans that, according to Belenky and others, "is one of the most complicated human achievements, requiring a high level of development. The individual who conceptualizes the self as basically connected to others sees the bonds that knit human relationships together as bonds of attachment" (178).

Motherhood, although addressed with mixed feelings, gave Brent a reason to struggle against her master, a reason to live.

When Dr. Flint came to her grandmother's house after the birth of her second child, to abuse her both physically and verbally, Brent states: "Had it not been for these ties to life, I should have been glad to be released by death, though I had lived only nineteen years" (78). The joys of motherhood, however, were always tempered for a slave mother by the knowledge that she could at any time be separated from her children. On the other hand, motherhood and the sense of self-in-connection induced Jacobs to try to escape slavery. Her master, in order to punish her, sent her with her small daughter to his son's plantation. There she engaged in the harshest chores and saw the true face of slavery. During her stay at the plantation she realized that her daughter had no future there and she says, "I felt how much easier it would be to see her die than to see her master beat her about, as I daily saw him beat other little ones" (87). Once she had returned her daughter to her grandmother's house and hidden herself from her master, she found it difficult to escape to the North. The dilemma is paradoxical, for "it is a distinctive feature of the outraged mother that she sacrifices opportunities to escape without her children" (Braxton, *Black* 33).

Jacobs's grandmother served as her source of strength and to whom she refers as her "great treasure." The loving relationship she shared with her grandmother gave her the strength to endure her confinement. Fox-Genovese states: "Black women's autobiographies abound with evidence of or references to the love that black female autobiographers felt for and felt from their female elders: mothers, aunts, grandmothers" ("Statue" 71). During her confinement Jacobs read, reflected, and developed the sense of self that enabled her to escape to the North. The sense of connection that is such an important aspect of Jacobs's narrative is not a part of Douglass's narrative. Douglass, unlike Jacobs, emphasizes his own transformation and isolation. According to William S. McFeely, Douglass, in his *Narrative*, isolates himself in his description of the confrontation with Mr. Covey, but "in isolating himself in order to point the moral, he was forgetting something that had been at the heart of the story, that Frederick Bailey—and Bill and Caroline—had worked out together on the Covey farm that August morning" (48). Jacobs never forgets the people who contribute to her development of self.

Jacobs made her escape to the North only after her children had been bought by their father and sent to New York to live. She was later reunited with both children. Her narrative reveals that she is "motivated by an overwhelming concern for the freedom and literacy of her children, a concern that is not apparent in the narratives of questing male slaves" (Braxton, *Black* 33). The existence of her children, while delaying her escape North, served to give Jacobs knowledge of herself as well as the courage and determination she needed to make her way to freedom. Jacob's narrative voice differs from that of male slave narrators in one other important area. She "celebrates the cooperation of all the people, slave and free, who make her freedom possible" (Braxton, *Black* 19). The image she presents is that of a web of relationships that develop and sustain her. These connections include not only her grandmother who hides her, her children who help her develop a sense of self, her brother who encourages and supports her, and other members of the slave community who aid in her escape, but also the friends who support and provide employment and traveling opportunities once she arrives first in New York and then in Boston. Belenky and others, in an interview with women from various ethnic and educational backgrounds, emphasize that "sustaining connections with others prevail in the stories of women" (84). The voice-in-relationship, the voice that emerges from a tightly woven web of connections with other people is the most powerful expression in Jacobs's narrative. This voice speaks against both slavery and patriarchy. Women are more likely than men to reveal a "relational self," for according to Catherine Keller, "women are less likely under the conditions of patriarchy to have repressed the fluidity and connectivity of which all persons consist" (202).

Chapter Two

Zora Neale Hurston's
Their Eyes Were Watching God

In her introduction to *Dust Tracks on a Road* (1942) Maya Angelou states: "It is difficult, if not impossible, to find and touch the real Zora Neale Hurston" (xii). Hurston's life has been surrounded by questions and controversy, and many of these questions, especially about her adult life, are not answered in her autobiography, *Dust Tracks on a Road*.

Of course, any autobiographical account is necessarily limited by the self that the autobiographer, both consciously and unconsciously, wishes to reveal. Elvin Holt states: "Writing an autobiography requires the author to select from a multitude of experiences those which most accurately reflect the self he wishes to project to his readers" (35). While it is true that parts of Hurston's personality and life will always remain elusive, she has selected certain experiences that appear repeatedly in her novels and nonfictional works. These experiences and perceptions disclose much of her personality; thus, Hurston reveals much more of herself than she probably ever intended.

Zora Neale Hurston's autobiography is contained in three volumes: her "official" autobiography, *Dust Tracks on a Road*; her famous anthropological work, *Mules and Men*; and her most famous novel, *Their Eyes Were Watching God*. Although *Their Eyes Were Watching God* is a work of fiction, it is autobiographical as well. Hurston reveals her personality through the narrative events and through the interplay of the author's, narrator's, and protagonist's voices. Not only does this book tell the reader about Hurston's life, but because it signifies upon or revises nineteenth century narratives written by African American women, it provides an important link between Harriet Jacobs's slave narrative and novels written by African American women in the last quarter of the twentieth century.

Their Eyes Were Watching God is the first self-conscious effort by an American ethnic writer not only to subvert patriarchal discourse but also to give voice to women of color. Mary Helen Washington states that Janie, Hurston's protagonist, "is one of the few—and certainly the earliest—heroic black woman in the Afro-American literary tradition" ("Woman" 16). Unlike literary foremothers such as Jessie Fauset, Frances E. W. Harper, and Pauline Hopkins, Hurston refuses either to stereotype Janie or to conform to earlier plot lines established by white predecessors. In her discussion of Harper's 1892 novel, *Iola Leroy*, Deborah E. McDowell describes the myth of the "true woman" which dominated white fiction and the countermyth that dominated African American fiction. The countermyth was tied to the notion of "uplifting" the entire African American race, was expressed through the "revisionist" fiction of the late nineteenth century, and was dominated by the "chaste" and pure African American heroine. The heroine of the countermyth is offered as a counterpart to the white heroine of the "cult of true womanhood." McDowell states:

> The countermyth dominates *Iola Leroy*. It is most striking in Iola's conscious choice to glorify the virtues of motherhood and domesticity, the mainstays of the mid-nineteenth-century cult of true womanhood ("Changing" 95).

While Harriet Jacobs gives "lip service" to the "cult of true womanhood" and later writers replace it with the countermyth, Hurston flatly rejects both the concept of the cult and its countermyth. In *Their Eyes Were Watching God*, Hurston signifies upon Jacobs's text as well as the countermyth, by moving her heroine, Janie, beyond the boundaries that restrained the "true woman."

Like Harriet Jacobs, Zora Neale Hurston was born in the South, but unlike Jacobs, she was born after the abolition of slavery and was raised in a community that was run by African Americans. Hurston was born in the all-black town of Eatonville, Florida about 1891.[1] Her mother died when Hurston was nine, and her death caused some dramatic changes in her daughter's life. Her father quickly remarried, but Hurston discovered an "adversary" in her stepmother (*Dust Tracks* 65-75). Because of the conflict with her stepmother, she left home at the age of fourteen to work as a lady's maid for a soprano in a traveling Gilbert and Sullivan operatic troupe. When the soprano, "Miss M," left the troupe to get married, Hurston found herself unemployed. She was determined to "be back in school," and with her brother's financial aid, she enrolled at Morgan Academy in Baltimore and then went on to Howard University in Washington D.C. Hurston received an Associate's Degree at Howard and studied intermittently there until 1924. She arrived in New York City in 1925 and became an integral part of the Harlem Renaissance. Soon after her arrival in New York City, she received a scholarship to attend Barnard College where she first met Franz Boaz, the man who later directed her work at Columbia University. Boaz not only inspired Hurston's work in anthropology but encouraged and supported her first trip back to Eatonville to do formal folklore research (*Dust Tracks* 85-125).

Although she came under the patronage of Mrs. Osgood Mason and received several fellowships and awards in the early years of her career, Hurston always had financial difficulties.[2] She worked hard and achieved several literary and dramatic successes, but she often could not afford necessities and was at least on one occasion "reduced to begging" Mrs. Mason for a pair of shoes. Despite physical and financial hardships, Hurston wrote and researched for thirty years and in that time she published four novels, two books of folklore, an autobiography, numerous stories, articles, and plays (Washington, "Woman" 13). Mary Helen Washington says of her life:

> She worked without the freedom and peace, without the time to contemplate, that Virginia Woolf insisted were essential for any woman to write. She worked consistently without the necessary five hundred pounds a year, without a room of her own with lock and key. Indeed, she worked most of the time without a door of her own on which to put a lock. What she left us is only a fraction of what she might have accomplished. We should be grateful for the work she did. We should be grateful for her survival ("Woman" 24).

Hurston undoubtedly lacked freedom, peace, and financial security throughout most of her career, but she did not lack energy, drive, or intellect. These latter three qualities enabled her to write *Their Eyes Were Watching God*. Hurston describes important events of her life in *Dust Tracks on a Road* (1942), in *Mules and Men* (1935), and in her letters and essays, but she best reveals her emotional development and personal commitments in her novel, *Their Eyes Were Watching God.*

Zora Neale Hurston wrote most of *Their Eyes Were Watching God* over a seven week period while she was in Haiti. She received a Guggenheim Fellowship and traveled to Haiti to collect data and write about the culture of the Caribbean. She often worked all day collecting anthropological data and then worked late into the night writing what would be her most famous novel. The impetus for such an outpouring of words was a love affair with Albert Price III, a young graduate student of West Indian descent whom she had left in New York. Although Price and Hurston married, they later divorced, and their relationship was strained during the period in which Hurston wrote her most famous novel. The conflict in Price's and Hurston's relationship evidently centered in two areas; the difference in their ages—he was twenty-three while she was over forty, and his objections to the intrusions of her career. In *Dust Tracks on a Road,* Hurston remembers: "But no matter how soaked we were in ecstasy, the telephone or the doorbell would ring, and there would be my career again. A charge had been laid upon me, and I must follow the call" (188). She also began to realize that the relationship would interfere with his career, for he was studying for the ministry. Although Hurston waited more than three years to end her marriage to Price, she realized as early as 1937 that a long-term relationship with Price was, in all probability, doomed. She concluded: "I have the satisfaction of knowing that I have loved and been loved by the perfect man. If I never hear of love again, I have known the real thing" (*Dust Tracks* 190).

The reader who knows Hurston's life can see connections between the fictional Janie of *Their Eyes* and Zora herself. Robert E. Hemenway states that *Their Eyes* is autobiographical of Hurston "only in the sense that she managed to capture the emotional essence of a love affair between an older woman and a younger man" (231). I, however, differ from Hemenway.

A close examination of the narrative and authorial voices of *Their Eyes* reveals that Hurston embodies much of her own emotional life in the creation of her protagonist, Janie

Crawford, Killicks, Starks, Woods. Hurston does not directly address her audience; the reader can, nevertheless, identify the author's voice. Booth states that authorial intrusion into a text is most easily identified through a prolonged "inside view" one has of a fictional character (*Rhetoric* 17). Barbara Christian considers Janie "a new black woman character. For the first time in black literature we feel the growing up of a black girl, not from without but from within" (*Black Women* 57). While Hurston provides the reader with an autobiographical "inside view," she also signifies on the earlier African American tradition represented by Harriet Jacobs, a tradition that did not provide a realistic, psychological development of protagonists. Jacobs is necessarily silent about her emotional and sexual development, Hurston not only discusses her "inside" development, but also tells the reader much about what it means to be an African American woman living in the United States in the 1930s.

The setting for Hurston's novel is her hometown of Eatonville, Florida; except for the names of the protagonists, the "fictional" Eatonville is difficult to distinguish from the "real" one. The owner of the store in Hurston's Eatonville was Joe Clarke, called "Jody" by his wife. The owner of the store in Janie's Eatonville is Joe Starks, whom Janie called "Jody." Although the resemblance between the real Mrs. Clarke and the fictional Mrs. Starks is minimal, both women worked in stores and were abused by their husbands. In both communities the porch of the town's store served as a meeting place for the exchange of ideas.

In *Dust Tracks* Hurston remembers that "Men sat around the store on boxes and benches and passed this world and the next one through their mouths" (45). In *Their Eyes* Hurston says that when "the people sat around on the porch and passed around the pictures of their thoughts for the others to look at and see, it was nice" (48). Janie discovered that the "people" who talked were men, and when the men began to pass around stories about the town's mule, she thought of stories she could tell, but her husband, Joe, "had forbidden her to indulge" (50). In *Dust Tracks* Hurston recalls that the stories she heard as a child, of God and the Devil and natural elements, "stirred up fancies in me" (51). Not only does Hurston call attention to the exclusion of women as story tellers, but she shows that they were really welcome only as an audience to validate and mirror male cleverness. In *Dust Tracks* women visited the store's porch "on Saturday nights and had it proven to the community that their husbands were good providers" (45). Hurston uses passive voice, ["had it proven"] in this passage to indicate that the women were objects, not active participants in the porch scene. Men objectify women in a somewhat similar manner in Hurston's novel. As three attractive women approach the porch, the men compete with one another for their attention. The men offer to buy the women anything they wish from the store. They also assure the women of their undying love. But everyone laughs at the men, for "It's acting-out courtship and everyone is in the play" (63). Of course, it is understood that the men are the actors, or subjects, in this play. Susanne Kappeler considers such self-expression "the project of the male cultural subject, and men have effectively usurped it as their exclusive prerogative through the very gendering of the roles of speaking and listening" (194). Sam and Lige, two of the "porch-talkers" demonstrate such gendering in their discourse. Sam tells Lige that they must have a subject, of their choosing of course, to address. He adds: "If uh man ain't got no bounds, he ain't got do place tuh stop" (*Their Eyes* 60). According to Diane Sadoff, "the porch tales reveal the men's insistence on female submission and inferiority, while they enhance masculine pride and encourage male solidarity" (16). In other words, the males on the porch have set the boundaries of discourse for the community.

Hurston takes her narrative a step further than Harriet Jacobs or any other pre-twentieth century female writer had done. While Linda Brent was limited to responding within the boundaries of discourse set by Dr. Flint, Janie actually disrupts the boundaries of Eatonville's male discourse. She not only challenges male and female roles in an effort to give her protagonist what Booth terms "freedom from" external restraints, but she also gives her protagonist, Janie Starks, "freedom to" speak against and ultimately transcend such restraints. "Every critical revolution tends to speak more clearly about what it opposes than about what it embraces" (*Company* 386). Hurston does both by giving her protagonist, Janie, the power to speak in a male dominated world. "Janie did what she had never done before, that is, thrust herself into the conversation" (70). She informs *her* male audience that not only does God get "'familiar wid us womenfolks too,'" but "'you don't know half as much 'bout us as you think you do'" (*Their Eyes* 70-71). The response, of course, is that Janie was getting "'too moufy,'" but this is an important moment in Janie's quest for self and voice. Janie moves, in two pages, from challenging the men on the porch to challenging her husband, Joe Starks, in the store. She stops the "laughter at the expense of women" and transforms it into laughter at the expense of her husband, laughter at the expense of men (*Their Eyes* 74-75). This is certainly a reversal of an almost universal patriarchal historical and literary tradition, a reversal that transcends the boundaries of Janie's ethnic community, the subversion of a tradition that comes from the mouth of the author herself. Thus, Hurston allows herself the "freedom to" laugh and to lie. In *Dust Tracks* Hurston speaks of her childhood friend who "pleased me always" (30). He was a white man who "would tell me what to do about things." His instruction was to always tell the truth: "don't you let me hear of you lying" (*Dust Tracks* 31). Yet Hurston brags of her ability to "lie", to tell tall stories, and generalizes: "Anybody whose mouth is cut cross-ways is given to lying, unconsciously as well as knowingly" (*Dust Tracks* 19). Hurston signifies upon Harriet Jacobs's inability to overtly challenge the "cult of true womanhood" by both subversively and overtly challenging gendered proscriptions against speech.

Hurston's voice can be heard as she relates the experiences of Janie's childhood and the structures of her subsequent relationships. The female autobiographer, in search of a new way of expressing herself within a patriarchal genre, "traces her origins to and through, rather than against, the mother whose presence has been repressed in order for the symbolic contract to emerge" (S. Smith 57). Hurston traces Janie's origins through her mother, Leafy, who was raped by the schoolmaster. Leafy abandoned her baby; consequently, Janie was raised by her grandmother, Nanny. Nanny, who was born into slavery, tells Janie that even though "De nigger woman is de mule uh de world," she had at one time "wanted to preach a great sermon about colored women sittin' on high" (*Their Eyes* 14).

Nanny was denied her pulpit, and freedom found her with a baby in her arms, so she tells Janie that she had planned great things for her daughter. After her daughter's life took a tragic turn, Nanny had placed all her hopes on her granddaughter, Janie. But Nanny had placed her hopes within the patriarchal system; therefore, she insisted that Janie marry Logan Killicks, a landowner, an older man who could protect her. Nanny failed to pass knowledge and self-identity to Janie, and for this Janie cannot forgive her.

Although Hurston traces her own origins through both parents, she tells the reader much more about her mother, Lucy Ann Potts, and her mother's family. "She who was considered the prettiest and the smartest black girl was throwing herself away and disgracing the Pottses by marrying an over-the-creek nigger, and a bastard at that" (*Dust Tracks* 8). Like Janie, Zora lost her mother at an early age. She considered the loss of her mother at the age of nine years "the end of a phase in my life" (*Dust Tracks* 64). "Mama died at sundown and changed a world. That is, the world which had been built out of her body and her heart" (*Dust Tracks* 65). The loss of a possible matriarchal world and the consequences of that loss reverberate throughout both Hurston's official autobiography, her autobiographical novel, and the precursor to that novel, Harriet Jacobs's *Incidents in the Life of a Slave Girl*.

Both Hurston and her protagonist, Janie, left their hometown and what was left of their families, and never went back. Hurston and Janie become wanderers; Hurston explains it through Janie: "sittin' still worries me. Ah wants tuh utilize mahself all over" (107). Hurston says of her mother's death: "That hour began my wanderings. Not so much in geography, but in time. Then not so much in time as in spirit" (*Dust Tracks* 64). The motif of the journey runs throughout African American narratives and is prefigured in most slave narratives, including Jacobs's *Incidents in the Life of a Slave Girl*. Janie leaves her hometown and first husband for Joe Starks but discovers that he wants only to put her on a pedestal, to make her an ornament, a testimony to his greatness. According to Sally Kitch, "For most of the twenty years of her marriage to Joe, Janie adopts silence as a survival strategy" (6). Once Janie finds her voice her "expressiveness becomes so powerful against male discourse that her language actually kills Joe" (Kitch 7).

While Hurston's discourse does not literally "kill" her husband, the man that inspired *Their Eyes*, her use of language, tied to her career as a writer and scholar, certainly played a part in ending this relationship. Hurston's voice is most certainly heard as Janie assesses her marriage to Joe Starks. When Janie married Joe Starks she was sure that "From now on until death she was going to have flower dust and springtime sprinkled over everything. A bee for her bloom"; however, Janie "wasn't petal-open" to Joe after he assured her that "All you got to do is mind me" (*Their Eyes* 31). "The spirit of the marriage left the bedroom and took to living in the parlor" (*Their Eyes* 66). Hurston describes her own relationship in similar terms. She remembers: "Who had canceled the well-advertised tour of the moon? Somebody had turned a hose on the sun. What I had taken for eternity turned out to be a moment walking in its sleep" (*Dust Tracks* 182).

One can also compare the language used to describe the younger man who inspired *Their Eyes* with the language used to describe the younger man with whom Janie fell in love. "Indeed many incidents between Janie and Jody, and Janie and Tea Cake are clearly transposed from Hurston's troubled relationship with A. W. Price" (Sadoff 20). Hurston recalls a conversation she had with her lover, A. W. Price. "I almost laughed out loud. That was just the way I felt. I hated to think of him smiling unless he was smiling at me. His grins were too precious to be wasted on ordinary mortals, especially women" (*Dust Tracks* 186). In *Their Eyes*, Janie and Tea Cake, the man who freed her to be herself, "made a lot of laughter out of nothing" (97). "They went inside and their laughter rang out first from the kitchen and all over the house" (102). There were, however, insecurities in both relationships. As Hurston's career began to make more demands on her, A. W. Price's insecurities surfaced. "He said once with pathos in his voice, that at times he could not feel my presence. My real self had escaped him" (*Dust Tracks* 188). Tea Cake likewise tells Janie: "Yo' face jus' left here and went off somewhere else" (*Their Eyes* 100).

Both Hurston and Janie sustain violence as a result of these insecurities. In *Dust Tracks*, however, Hurston's voice excuses the conflict and attempts to soften the blows. She relates an incident in which she slapped Price's face. "He paid me off then and there with interest. No broken bones, you understand, and black eyes." Hurston explains this behavior as rooted in insecurity and caused by a casual kiss by an old friend (*Dust Tracks* 187). Tea Cake is also jealous and fearful of another man. "Before the week was over he had whipped Janie. Not because her behavior justified his jealousy, but it relieved that awful fear inside him. No brutal beating at all" (*Their Eyes* 140). Although Hurston's surface voice excuses the jealousies and violence, "the committed writer's ambivalence about heterosexual relationships betrays itself in her choice of language to describe her novel's genesis; it 'embalms' her passion—kills and preserves it" (Sadoff 20). After Tea Cake beats Janie, "God" intervenes in the form of a flood. It is the flood and the bite from a rabid animal that causes Janie to have to kill Tea Cake. Dianne Sadoff considers Janie a "dangerous woman" because she metaphorically kills her second husband with her language and literally, albeit unintentionally, kills her third. "Hurston has motivated her narrative, perhaps unconsciously, to act out her rage against male domination and to free Janie, a figure for herself, from all men" (Sadoff 22). While Harriet Jacobs experienced violence at the hands of her master, Janie and Hurston experience it at the hands of their husbands. These instances of violence can be considered the obverse images of patriarchy.

Violence and attempted male domination were a part of Hurston's world. bell hooks points out that Hurston "calls attention to the way in which male notions of female inferiority must be continually reaffirmed by active aggression" (14). Hurston does call attention to male aggression and violence in *Dust Tracks*, but she also records instances of female aggression. When her Uncle Jim bought a pair of shoes and then presented them to another woman, Hurston's Aunt Caroline marched through the town after him with an axe "draped over her shoulder" and managed to retrieve the shoes (*Dust Tracks* 15). The women of Hurston's community, unlike women created within the confines of the "cult of true womanhood" or the African American countermyth, were never submissive or passive victims of masculine abuse. While hooks sees "new paradigms for heterosexual bonding" presented in the relationship between Janie and Tea Cake in *Their Eyes Were Watch-*

ing God, the masculine, aggressive stance Tea Cake assumes undermines the fulfillment of that bonding (15). Hurston suggests new paradigms for heterosexual relationships, but these paradigms are not fully developed, nor are they applied to society as a whole. Tea Cake, like all of Hurston's men, fails to reach the self-reflexiveness that eventually becomes a part of Janie's personality.

Hurston fought with other insecurities related to A. W. Price, the man who inspired *Their Eyes Were Watching God*. She evidently felt quite self-conscious about the gap in their ages. The very first discussion that the community has regarding Janie involves her age. When Janie comes walking back into town one of the first accusations hurled at her is that she is an "ole woman." When her friend Pheoby defends her as not "so ole as some of y'all dat's talking," the community's voice retorts that "she's way past forty" (3). While the "gap" in Janie's and Tea Cake's ages is placed at twelve years, evidently the gap in Hurston's and Price's ages was greater. Price was twenty-three and Hurston, at the time, claimed to be thirty-seven. Arnold Rampersad states, however, that "Hurston was born in the black town of Eatonville, Florida, on January 7, 1891—but so willfully misrepresented herself later that even her diligent biographer believed that her year of birth was 1901" (*Mules and Men* xix). This willful misrepresentation might explain Hurston's comments about "lying" as well as her preoccupation with Janie's age in *Their Eyes*. It is true that Janie returns home alone, finally her own woman, and "pulled in her horizon like a fish-net" and "called in her soul" (*Their Eyes* 184). According to Alice Walker, Zora like Janie, returned home to Florida near the end of her life. She lived alone and for some time supported herself by working as a maid for a white family in central Florida. She worked on a novel about Herod, but was never able to finish it, and she ended her days as a resident of the St. Lucie County, Florida, Welfare Home in January, 1959. She was buried in an unmarked grave in Fort Pierce, Florida and almost totally forgotten until Alice Walker, thirteen years later, made a trip to Florida to place a marker on her grave (*Search* 93-113).

As an omniscient author, Hurston allows her people to speak and act for themselves, but she also reveals what is going on in the minds of her characters and speaks to their mental states. Norman Friedman states that such an author tends to reveal the inward thoughts of these characters "to the reader in his own voice. Similarly, the mental states and the settings which evoke them are *narrated* indirectly as if they have already occurred—discussed, analyzed and explained—rather than presented *scenically* as if they were occurring now" (Friedman 1172). There are several instances in *Their Eyes* in which Janie's mental state is thus explained. The very first sentence of Chapter 2 reveals Janie's thoughts as a young girl in just such a manner: "Janie saw her life like a great tree in leaf with the things suffered, things enjoyed, things done and undone. Dawn and doom was in the branches" (8). Later, after Janie is married to Joe Starks, Hurston's voice is heard thinking through her protagonist once more: "Sometimes she stuck out into the future, imagining her life different from what it was. But mostly she lived between her hat and her heels, with her emotional disturbances like shade patterns in the woods—come and gone with the sun" (*Their Eyes* 72). Finally, after Joe's death, Janie discovers her true worth and Hurston presents it to the reader as follows: "She had found a jewel down inside herself and she had wanted to walk where people could see her and gleam it around" (*Their Eyes* 86). In each of these examples, Janie's mental state is presented to the reader as if it had already occurred. In the last example, especially, Janie's thoughts are presented to the reader in the past perfect tense, indicating that these are thoughts from the past, thoughts given expression through the authorial voice.

The authorial voice can be identified in at least one other way. Hurston's voice can also be identified by locating her obsessions, the images and metaphors that occur repeatedly in her texts. Richard Hugo distinguishes between the "public" and the "private" poet. Like Harriet Jacobs, Hurston can be considered a public poet, for the intellectual and emotional content of the words of a public poet are the same for writer and reader. A private poet or author uses certain images and words repeatedly that "mean something to the poet they don't mean to the reader" (14). Hugo calls these images "triggering subjects," and says although the reader can identify these images and words she/he cannot ascertain exactly what they mean to the author (15). Hurston personifies an image of Death that appears in both *Their Eyes* and *Dust Tracks*. In *Their Eyes* Death was "that strange being with the huge square toes who lived way in the West. The great one who lived in the straight house like a platform without sides to it, and without a roof" (79). Death stands in this house "with his sword drawn back, waiting for the messenger to bid him come" (80). Death is not a welcome figure in any of these images. Joe Starks waged a battle with Death and lost when "the icy sword of the square-toed one had cut off his breath" (82). Hurston includes a similar description of "Old Death" in *Dust Tracks* when she tells of the death of her mother. She says that the "Master-Maker" made him with "big, soft feet and square toes" and made "a weapon for his hand to satisfy his needs" (63). In *Dust Tracks* Death dwells on a platform much like the one Hurston describes in *Their Eyes* with an important exception. In *Dust Tracks* Death lives "in his secret place in our yard" (63). Death is also much more polite to Hurston's mother than he is to Joe Starks; in *Dust Tracks* he "bowed to Mama in his way, and she made her manners and left us to act out our ceremonies over unimportant things" (64). Even though Death is more polite in *Dust Tracks*, the reader is aware of his sword and that often it involved a struggle that could appear to be "the end of a war" (*Their Eyes* 56). Booth states that "Every weapon metaphor implies a world in which the question of winning or losing is primary" (*Company* 309). Although the reader can never know all the emotions Hurston felt regarding Death, her obsession with the subject, her personification of Death, and her notion of struggle and ultimate defeat brought by the sword of Death all give the reader insight into Hurston's world. Cyrena N. Pondrom states that the cyclic (indeed, infinite) structure of *Their Eyes* is revealed in Hurston's obsessions with death and resurrection, for the opening lines of the novel follow the burying of Tea Cake. Within the imagery of the opening lines, Janie's vitality is portrayed as "a triumph of life over death" (187).

Another obsession of Hurston's is the subject of God and religion. Hurston devotes an entire chapter of *Dust Tracks* to the subject of religion. She discusses her father's role as minister to the church, describes the church services, and then explains why she sees religion in more universal terms: "I have made my peace with the universe as I find it, and bow to its laws" (202). During the hurricane in *Their Eyes*, Hurston describes the power of nature and the universe: "They seemed to be staring at the dark, but their eyes were watching God" (151). At the conclusion of *Their Eyes*, Janie tells her friend, Phoeby, that there are two things everybody must do for themselves. "They got tuh go tuh God, and they got tuh find out about livin' fuh theyselves" (183). While Hurston signifies upon Harriet Jacobs's view of religion by moving outside the boundaries of traditional religion, she fails to designate the specifics of her religious beliefs.

Hurston's obsession with religion and myth found expression in her work as an anthropologist. In *Mules and Men* she collected the folklore and myths of the African American culture of the South. Wendy Doniger O'Flaherty defines anthropologists as those "who do not usually travel in time," but who "travel far in space, to the farthest reaches of Otherness" (12). Hurston herself spoke from these far "reaches of Otherness." As a college-educated African American returning to her own community to collect data on the Other, and as a woman who spoke from the periphery of Otherness from within the community, she gives new meaning to the mythos of her community.

According to O'Flaherty "all truly creative scholarship in the humanities is autobiographical, but it is particularly evident that people who traffic in myths are caught up in them" (13). Hurston was most certainly "caught up" in the myths she collected, for many of them appear in her autobiographical writings. These myths are reinterpreted or retranslated by Hurston to reveal the position of women within the African American community. One of the mule stories that Hurston collected in *Mules and Men* is the story of "The Talking Mule." It is unexpected for a mule to talk, so unexpected that when *she* does, the farmer runs out of the country (172-173). While women serve as metaphorical mules in *Their Eyes*, the porch-sitters, the men of Eatonville were "mule-talkers." They discussed Matt Bonner's mule every day. Matt Bonner had mistreated his mule, had overworked him, had starved him, and finally, one day, the mule left home. The porch-sitters, the men, were teasing and tormenting both Matt and the mule. "Every-body was having fun at the mule-baiting. All but Janie. A little war of defense for helpless things was going on inside her" (*Their Eyes* 53). Joe Starks buys the mule after he overhears Janie talking to herself, and he sets the mule free. Janie thanks him publicly for his act of kindness and likens it to Lincoln's freeing the slaves (*Their Eyes* 55). Like the mule's speech, Janie's talk is unexpected, and her speech, like the unexpected speech of the mule, eventually defeats Joe's "big voice." Janie meta-phorically runs both Joe and the porch talkers "out of the coun-try." The mule is the Other and Hurston's voice, through Janie, speaks in defense of this Other, as mule, as black, and as woman. Janie's voice in *Their Eyes* is as unexpected as Linda Brent's when she "sasses" Dr. Flint in *Incidents*, but serves much the same purpose, for it is used to challenge and ultimately defeat the power that enslaves it.

Hurston as anthropologist speaks through another incident connected to the mule story. The freed mule entertains the town of Eatonville with his antics and provides many more mule "lies" for the talkers, but eventually, the mule dies. The townspeople decide to have a "dragging out," to the swamp, a mock-funeral for the dead mule. Janie is excited about the occasion, but Joe forbids her to go. "But de Mayor's wife is somethin' different again. But *you* ain't goin' off in all dat mess uh commoness" (*Their Eyes* 56). At the funeral, Joe speaks of mule heaven and mule-angels, and sweet revenge on Matt Bonner. After the townspeople leave, the buzzards swoop in for their feast. This part of the narrative is considered by many critics to be quite a departure from the realism that character-izes *Their Eyes*. Henry L. Gates Jr. states:

> This allegory, shatters completely any illusion the reader might have had that this was meant to be a realistic fiction, even though the text has naturalized the possibility of such an event occurring, if only by representing storytelling in direct speech as its principal mode of narration (201).

Gates correctly sees the allegory of the buzzards as a ritual that signifies upon the mock funeral. It can also be heard as an expression of Hurston's anthropological and womanist voice. As an anthropologist, Hurston was concerned to relate the

folktales of her people. As a "womanist" her voice reflected
the definition later recorded by Alice Walker. Walker traces
the term "womanist" from the black folk expression of mothers to their daughters, "'You acting womanish,' i.e., like a
woman. Usually referring to outrageous, audacious, courageous
or *willful* behavior" (*Search* xi). The term is also a reflection of
black feminism. Hurston's voice is audacious, courageous and
feminist as she uses the buzzards to signify upon the mock
funeral. Just as the dragging out of the mule and the mock
funeral that follows is dominated by the men of Eatonville and
Joe Starks's "big voice," the meeting of the buzzards tropes,
through parody, the dominance of the patriarchal structure it
reflects. And, Hurston's audacious "womanist" voice siginifies
upon that of her predecessor, Harriet Jacobs.

Hurston presents the allegory of the buzzards in the form
of a myth. After the people leave the dead mule, the buzzards
who were "holding a great flying-meet way up over the heads
of the mourners" began to move in, but they had to wait until
their white-headed leader, the Parson, alighted and gave them
the signal to begin the feast (*Their Eyes* 57). The Parson slowly
moved into the vicinity, examined the body, and then held a
mock funeral punctuated by the call-and-response ritual of
African American church meetings (*Their Eyes* 58). According
to O'Flaherty, "Though animals may express the most intimate
and primal sides of our own natures, what is most deeply *us*,
they may also represent the extremes of otherness, human
strangers (barbarians and foreigners) or gods" (80). Talking
animals are a very common element of African American culture. Of the sixty-nine folktales or pseudomyths in *Mules and
Men*, at least twenty of them involve animals who talk with
people or with each other. The purpose of these talking animals is to comment on their human counterparts. The funeral
is a parody on the religious ritual of call-and-response, a parody
that focuses the reader's attention on the patriarchal structure
of the church and the community.

As an anthropologist Hurston was always dealing with the
myths of society. For example, since naming is an important
aspect of African and African American culture, it is very likely
that Hurston gave Janie's mother the name Leafy from her
knowledge of myths. "In many Greek and Roman myths the

sexually assaulted woman is permanently transformed into a plant or an animal" (O'Flaherty *Dreams* 99). After Callisto was seduced by Jupiter, she was transformed into a bear, and Io was transformed into a cow. Lotis was transformed into a lotus tree as she fled from the lust of Priapus; similarly, Daphne was transformed into a tree as she fled from Phoebus.[3] Janie's grandmother, Nanny, is not named from myth, but after she saw Janie kissing Johnny Taylor her "head and face looked like the standing roots of some old tree that had been torn away by storm" (*Their Eyes* 12). As a slave, Nanny had been sexually assaulted by her master. Her image as a tree recalls transformations that served to preserve the integrity and strength of ancient women. Like Callisto, whose mind remained unchanged after her body had been transformed, Nanny, even as a slave, determined to provide "a highway through the wilderness" for her offspring (*Their Eyes* 15). After she gave birth to her daughter, Leafy, she was abused by her jealous mistress. Unlike mythic women who were rooted to one spot in their transformations, Nanny tells Janie that slavery transformed "us colored folks" into "branches without roots" (*Their Eyes* 15). This lack of roots kept Nanny from fulfilling her own dreams, but, like transformed mythic women, she determined to provide for her descendants. The tree itself is a symbol of endurance and power and occurs repeatedly as such throughout the writings of both nineteenth and twentieth century African American women.

Hurston may also have drawn from myth for her shadow image of Janie. After Janie's image of Joe Starks tumbled off the shelf inside her, she realized that she had an inside and an outside, "and suddenly she knew how not to mix them" (*Their Eyes* 68). Janie became a shadow woman as "she sat and watched the shadow of herself going about tending store and prostrating itself before Jody, while all the time she herself sat under a shady tree with the wind blowing through her hair and her clothes" (*Their Eyes* 73). Shadow women exist in Indian myths in which raped women are "often permanently transformed into a goddess or into some supernatural creature who is literally a shadow of herself . . . the woman's shadow may begin as an ephemeral creature but go on to endure alongside the original or even take over the central role" (O'Flaherty *Dreams* 99). Janie was not raped but she was verbally abused by Joe. She transferred her emotional existence into her shadow, and after Joe's death, this is the woman who took over the central role and began to speak for herself. Pondrom describes Janie as an "Ur-woman," a "survivor of the Flood. Like Ishtar, she has harrowed Hell and escaped to tell the tale" (187).[4]

Just as Harriet Jacobs subverted the myth of true womanhood, as a black female anthropologist Hurston could subvert myths by interpreting them from a womanist point of view. According to O'Flaherty, "There *is* no myth devoid of interpretation; the choice of the words in which to tell it begins the process of interpretation" (31). Hurston subverts the patriarchal autobiographical form in *Dust Tracks*, according to Claudine Raynaud,

> by using competing discourses—folkloric material, tall tales, residual structure from the spiritual autobiography. Hurston's ease in the persona of the folklorist proves that the anthropological relationship between the black female anthropologist and the white reader is always safer, and potentially more subversive (131).

While Harriet Jacobs simply adopted the patriarchal autobiographical form to inform her reader, Hurston signifies upon the form itself by using competing discourses to subvert the patriarchal interpretation of myths in *Their Eyes*. Hurston does more than subvert this interpretation. She creates a powerful female figure in Janie, and through her, a powerful female myth.

Unlike the narrator of Jacobs's *Incidents in the Life of a Slave Girl*, the narrators of *Their Eyes* are somewhat distanced from the text. In addition to narrators of short embedded narratives, the reader can identify two main narrators of *Their Eyes Were Watching God*. Lanser would characterize one as a public narrator who addresses a private audience, she would consider the other a private narrator who addresses a specific narratee (*Narrative Act* 133). The public narrator is omnipotent and as such has the ability to speak in a detached voice in formal language, to recreate the voices and thoughts of the character-actors, to adopt the dialect used by the character-actors, and to incorporate part or all of it into her voice. In other words, the public narrator of *Their Eyes* serves as a multivoiced creator and authority within the story world.[5] *Their Eyes* can be described as a formal text characterized by a "narrative unconsciousness" in which the narrator, unlike the narrator of *Incidents in the Life of a Slave Girl*, never speaks about the narrative act (Lanser, *Narrative Act* 178). The public narratee can best be described as a "degree zero passive narratee," one who is never directly or indirectly addressed (Lanser, *Narrative Act* 182). Although this narrator's voice is not as directly accessible as Linda Brent's in Jacobs's *Incidents*, the reader can identify her gender and perspective.

While the public narrator of *Their Eyes* is "unmarked"—that is, there are no indications within the text as to sex—the reader can assume that the narrator is female. The reader becomes aware of the narrator's sex because her sympathy and closest identification is with Janie, the female protagonist who embarks on a search for self knowledge. The narrator announces on the first page of the book that "the beginning of this was a woman," in order to let the reader know that the perspective is female (*Their Eyes* 1). The narrator's voice insures that the reader will identify and sympathize with Janie, because it is primarily through her consciousness that the story unfolds. The voice of the narrator, whether speaking through Janie, or on her own, however, always speaks as a female.

A narrative text is composed of two areas of discourse, that of the narrator(s) and that of the characters. The narrator of *Their Eyes* makes use of free indirect discourse, where "the narrator adopts the tone or phraseology of a character, incorporating it within the narrator's own speech activity," and conversely, "the narrator's speech infiltrates the character's discourse . . . where the thoughts, words, or perceptions represented are those of the character, but the syntax is that of the narrative voice" (Lanser, *Narrative Act* 186). Suzanne Fleischman further distinguishes free indirect discourse by

> the presence of features of (direct speech questions, exclamations, fragments, repetitions, deictics, emotive and conative words, overstatements, colloquialisms) reported in the fashion of indirect speech, i.e., with third-person pronouns and shifted tenses, but normally without the characteristic inquit formulas such as "X said/thought that . . ., wondered why . . ." (227).

The narrator of *Their Eyes* adopts the speech patterns used by the community of Eatonville as she describes the growing relationship between Janie and Tea Cake. "Done quit attending

church, like she used to. Gone off to Sanford in a car with Tea
Cake and her all dressed in blue! It was a shame. Done took to
high heel slippers and a ten dollar hat!" (105). Hurston signifies upon earlier patterns of discourse and dialogue that are
represented in Harriet Jacobs's narrative by capturing not only
the speech of the community but also the thought processes
of Janie and incorporating them into free indirect discourse.

Perhaps the most interesting aspect of free indirect discourse
is that it blurs not only the boundary between the protagonist
and narrator, but it also blurs the boundary between free indirect *speech* and free indirect *thought*. Free indirect speech moves
away from the actual language of either the narrator or protagonist, while free indirect thought "involves a move toward
language" (Fleischman 228). Free indirect thought processes
seem to be more under the control of the protagonist, while
free indirect speech proceeds from the narrator. In *Their Eyes*
Janie's thought process is captured as she worries about Tea
Cake's absence: "But oh God, don't let Tea Cake be off somewhere hurt and Ah not know nothing about it. And God, please
suh, don't let him love nobody else but me" (115). Janie's
thoughts closely resemble her speech pattern, but her thoughts
are not set apart by quotation marks or "inquit" formulas. Maria
Tai Wolff states that "the book's narration is deliberately flexible; it takes on the qualities suitable to the situation it describes" (33). Gates credits Hurston with introducing free indirect discourse into African American narration (191). The
purpose of this study is to show that the narrators of *Their Eyes*
do not shift points of view or move from spectator to partici-
pant,[6] but rather, dual voices often speak through the narrative consciousness to express not only the African American
mode of storytelling in dialect, but also the polyphony associated with both African American and feminist perspective.

The formal voice of the public narrator is the first to speak
in *Their Eyes*. Her immediate purpose is to tell the reader the
difference between the dreams of men and women. Men's
dreams are like ships on the far horizon; for some, the ships
come in with the tide, but other men's ships never land, "until
the Watcher turns his eyes away in resignation, his dreams
mocked to death by Time." The narrator tells the reader that
women "forget all those things they don't want to remember"

that for them "the dream is the truth" (*Their Eyes* 1). She then introduces the reader to Janie Woods, the woman whose story this is. After introducing the story and the woman, the narrator "focalizes" through the community. In this instance the community "functions as a kind of medium, which the narrator 'inhabits' in order to be 'on the scene' or 'in the mind' of a character, but no independence of voice necessarily accompanies this focalizing privilege" (Lanser, *Narrative Act* 142). The narrator thus moves from impartial witness and philosopher to privileged seer, and does so at the beginning of the story so the reader expects the narrator to speak through the minds of the character-actors throughout the narrative. Earlier slave narratives, such as Harriet Jacobs's were focalized only through one mind and one voice. By focalizing through the minds of the African American community, Hurston not only signifies upon earlier narratives, but creates a much more powerful narrative voice.

Even though the narrator is inside the minds of the people who are witnessing the return of Janie Woods, the reader is aware that the narrator is not in sympathy with their thoughts. The people are first introduced as "skins" who "felt powerful and human," who make "killing tools out of laughs," and engage in "mass cruelty." The narrator distinguishes between the envious thoughts of the men and women on the porch. As Janie walks in front of the porch, the men proceed to mentally undress her. "They, the men, were saving with the mind what they lost with the eye" (*Their Eyes* 1). The women, on the other hand noticed her "faded shirt and muddy overalls and laid them away for remembrance" (*Their Eyes* 2). The narrator is once again distinguishing between the perceptions of men and women, and informing the reader that she is not in sympathy with the community. One wonders if Hurston had encountered or at least witnessed similar criticism from the actual community of Eatonville in which she was raised.

After revealing the thoughts of the "skins" on the porch, the narrator adopts the dialect of the community. She allows the community to speak so the reader may know its opinion of Janie. "'She de one been doin' wrong'" (3). The community's voice gives way to a conversation between the protagonist, Janie, and her best friend, Pheoby. Janie is full of "self-revelation" and offers to tell Pheoby the story of her life. Before the second level of narration begins, however, the public narrator moves from impartial eyewitness to involved observer. She states: "Time makes everything old so the kissing, young darkness became a monstropolous old thing while Janie talked" (*Their Eyes* 7). The use of the word "monstropolous," a word that Janie might use, brings the reader into close proximity of Janie's mind. The introduction of language used by the protagonist into the narrative account is termed "psychonarration" by Dorrit Cohn, an instance in which the thoughts and feelings of the character are filtered through the narrator's consciousness. Psychonarration is "the narrator's discourse about a character's consciousness" (Cohn 14). The narrator's voice may adopt the words and temporal perspective of the character, but the consciousness and most of the discourse belongs to the narrator. This type of discourse occurs repeatedly in *Their Eyes*, bringing the narrative and authorial voices into close proximity. In this case, the use of Janie's language is a transition into Janie's narrative.

Before Janie begins to speak the narrator makes one statement that likens Janie's life to a great tree, an image that recurs repeatedly in the text.[7] Then, Janie begins her story which she tells to Pheoby. Janie can be considered the private narrator of *Their Eyes*, since she functions within the story as the protagonist and tells her story to a narratee who also functions within the story. It is significant that Janie tells her story to another woman, since it is considered traditionally correct for women to speak or write to other women. Unlike Harriet Jacobs who wrote to northern white women and who pleaded for sympathy and understanding, Janie tells her story to another African American woman who is already in sympathy with her and who is eager to hear her story. According to Dale Spender, "there is no contradiction in patriarchal order while women write for women and therefore remain within the limits of the private sphere; the contradiction arises only when women write (or speak) for men" (192). Pheoby's role, as a receptive narratee, assures the validation and authority of Janie's voice. Janie tells Pheoby about her early childhood, her mother's tragic life, and her grandmother. Her grandmother, Nanny, worked as a servant for the Washburns and lived in a house in the back. Janie, who played with the Washburns' grand-children, tells Pheoby that "Ah didn't know Ah wuzn't white till Ah was round six years old" (8). Janie's lack of self-aware-ness as a child reflects Harriet Jacobs's slave narrative. Jacobs states that, "I was born a slave; but I never knew it till six years of happy childhood had passed away" (*Incidents* 5). Like Linda Brent, Janie lacks an accurate image of herself as a child. She also fails to envision new paradigms for African American women, and therefore conforms to society's demands. More than half a century after the publication of *Their Eyes* an Afri-can American protagonist, Alice Walker's Celie, proposes new paradigms for women's lives.

The public narrator allows Janie to narrate briefly, but then her voices speak for the remainder of the text, although they always move toward convergence with Janie's voice. Janie re-members that "her conscious life had commenced at Nanny's gate" (*Their Eyes* 10). This memory is the frame of the novel; while the narrator allows her to speak briefly for herself, her narrative is quickly taken over by the public narrator. Although the narration switches from Janie's voice to the primary or public narrator's, this time the voice is heard from within Janie's mind as the narrator recounts Janie's search for self and voice. Janie remembers when her conscious life began (10). She sees and experiences sexual ecstacy, but the voice of it all is "inau-dible" (10). She begins "seeking confirmation of the voice and vision" and find answers "for all other creations except her-self" (11). She tries kissing Johnny Taylor, but when her grand-mother sees her, her childhood ends. Her grandmother calls her into the house where the formal narrative voice is only occasionally interjected into the dialogue. Gates characterizes this narrative voice as follows:

> When such narrative commentary does surface, it often serves to func-tion as stage direction rather than as a traditional omniscient voice, as if to underscore Hurston's contention that it is 'drama' that 'per-meates [the Negro's] entire self,' and it is the dramatic to which black oral narration aspires" (199).

The use of free indirect discourse within *Their Eyes* signifies upon Harriet Jacob's narrative, for Jacobs's formal, educated voice dominates her narrative. Jacobs's use of dialect does not connect her narrator with her protagonists, but actually distances her protagonist, Linda Brent, from the rest of the African American community in Edenton, North Carolina.

Nanny tells Janie that she is a woman, that "de nigger woman is de mule uh de world," and that she must marry Logan Killicks for "protection" (14). She tells Janie that she once had dreams, but her dreams "about colored women sittin' on high" never materialized. The narrator provides an "inside view" of Nanny as she prepares to tell Janie her slave narrative. "The 'white man thinks in a written language,' Hurston claims, while 'the Negro thinks in hieroglyphics'" (Gates 199). "Mind-pictures brought feelings, and feelings dragged out drama from the hollows of her heart" (16). Nanny tells a story of failed hopes and dreams, and Nanny ends her dialogue by entreating Janie to obey her wishes. She asks Janie to treat her gently for "'Ah'm a cracked plate'" (19). Although Nanny's slave narrative ends on a note of hopelessness, Janie's narrative embodies much of the hope expressed by African Americans who were one generation removed from slavery.

The public narrator continues her psychonarration of Janie and Nanny in Chapter Three of *Their Eyes*. Janie asks questions about love, marriage and the end to loneliness, and she then marries Logan Killicks. "The new moon had been up and down three times before she got worried in mind" (21). She confronts her grandmother with her feelings, but her grandmother refuses to comfort her. The narrator tells the reader, however, that Nanny was deeply disturbed over the confrontation: "Then there is a depth of thought untouched by words, and deeper still a gulf of formless feeling untouched by thought. Nanny entered this infinity of conscious pain again on her knees" (23). Nanny dies soon after this. The narrator then shows the reader some of the "mind-pictures" inside Janie. Janie knew "things that nobody had ever told her." "She knew the world was a stallion rolling in the blue pasture of ether. She knew that God tore down the old world every evening and built a new one by sun-up. She knew now that marriage did not make love" (24). While the narrator shows limited sympathy for Nanny, it is on Janie's growing consciousness that she focuses in a particularly empathetic manner. The interplay of complex narrative metaphors with free indirect discourse not only reflects Janie's intuitive knowledge and creative capacity but also provides a sense of connection between the narrator's and protagonist's voices.

The public narrator informs the reader that since Janie's first dream was dead and all the familiar things and people had failed her, she began to look "up the road towards way off" (24). This is how she meets Joe Starks. The narrator uses the method of free indirect discourse for the first time to introduce the reader to Joe Starks. According to hooks, "Hurston's portrait of Joe Starks is initially flattering, becoming progressively negative as his character unfolds" (13). Starks, like all of Janie's husbands is eventually portrayed as insanely egotistical. In an extended paragraph, she uses the dialect that Joe himself would have used and tells the audience that his ambition is to become a "big voice" in a town in "Floridy" that has been built by "colored folks" (27). The use of free indirect discourse and idiomatic black voice in this passage provides a kind of "inside view" of Joe. While it is not as complete as the psychonarration of Janie and Nanny, by adopting a voice much like Joe's, the narrator allows much more of his personality to be revealed. The paragraph and the dialogue that follows is focalized through Joe as he shifts his attention from himself to Janie and finally concludes: "'A pretty doll-baby lak you is made to sit on de front porch and rock and fan yo'self and eat p'taters dat other folks plant just special for you'" (28). Although the narrator focalizes through Joe's consciousness, any sense of connection between Joe's voice and the narrative voice is absent. While the narrator does not focalize through Janie's speech in the first half of *Their Eyes*, she empathetically introduces Janie's consciousness into the narrative through free indirect discourse or psychonarration.

The narrator reveals her ideological stance in Chapter Five. The power and presence of speech and its role in gender relations is the focus of this chapter. Janie realizes that she is not attracted to Joe but "he spoke for far horizon," and so she leaves Killicks to start a new life with Joe Starks (29). She also realizes that "Her old thoughts were going to come in handy now, but new words would have to be made and said to fit them" (31). Janie is not allowed to say these new words, however. Joe, who regularly punctuates his discourse with "I god," effectively silences her. Joe is made Mayor of Eatonville, but when it is proposed that Mrs. Mayor Starks make a speech, Joe cuts it short. He announces "mah wife don't know nothin' 'bout no speech-makin.' Ah never married her for nothin' lak dat. She's uh woman and her place is in de home." This is what "took the bloom off of things" and left Janie "feeling cold" (41). When Janie and Joe arrive in Eatonville, the first inhabitants they meet are Amos Hicks and Lee Coker. Hicks and Coker are surprised by the "tone" of Starks's voice and the beauty of his wife. Lee Coker comments: "'Dat man talks like a section foreman'" (33). Hicks responds that he plans to go to Georgia to get a wife like Janie. Although he lacks money, he plans to get a wife with his talk. He claims that women love to hear him talk "'because dey can't understand it. Mah co-talkin' is too deep. Too much co to it'" (34). The narrator not only reveals the male preoccupation with voice and power, but she also gives an example of closure that women have traditionally used. When Hicks tries to "co-talk" Janie, he is met first with silence. When he pushes Janie to talk with, "'Folks must be mighty close-mouthed where you come from,'" Janie responds, "'Dat's right. But it must be different at yo' home'" (35). This is not only the first example of Janie's ability to signify, but in making Hicks appear foolish, the narrator undercuts the male argument of superior intellect. Although Janie is unable to overcome Joe's domination of her as easily as she silences Amos Hicks, the narrator reveals Janie's determination to resist condescending, sexist behavior.

Janie's consciousness continues to grow during the years she was married to Joe. She worked in the store with him, and she hated it, but she obeyed him. At his command, she even tied her long hair in a head-rag, a situation which irked her tremendously. In her discussion of the head-rag episode, the narrator offers more of an inside view of Joe's mind. This is the first instance of psychonarration with Joe Starks. The narrator reveals that Joe had Janie tie her hair up because he had imagined seeing the other men in the store running their hands through it. He ordered her to tie it up but refused to tell her why. "She was there in the store for *him* to look at not those others. But he never said things like that it just wasn't it him" (52). The narrator is questioning Joe's possessiveness as well as his conviction that men didn't need to verbalize their feelings. After the dragging out of the mule, the narrator also enters Joe's mind. He is resentful that Janie did not appreciate his efforts on her behalf. "She wasn't even appreciative of his efforts and she had plenty cause to be. Here he was just pouring honor all over her; building a high chair for her to sit in and overlook the world and she here pouting over it!" (59). Unlike the psychonarrations of Nanny and Janie, there is not even limited sympathy for Joe in these views. The inside view of Joe's mind only serves to show the growing distance between Janie and Joe and to reveal Joe's limited ability to communicate or sympathize with Janie or with any woman. Indeed, the narrator's purpose is quite simply to show the limitations of Joe's mind. Again, Hurston's use of psychonarration and free indirect discourse to enter the minds of the protagonists is a revision of earlier nineteenth century narratives.

The narrator informs the reader that Janie ceased to be "petal-open" with Joe. Scenes such as the one in which Joe told her that "Somebody got to think for women and chillun and chickens and cows. I god, they sho don't think none theirselves," made Janie think about the "inside state of her marriage. Finally, Joe's image fell off the shelf and Janie realized "She had an inside and an outside now and suddenly she knew how not to mix them" (67). Soon after this realization Janie begins to find her voice. The narrator uses the casual conversation of the men on the porch to reveal their sexism. The favorite topics of these men are the stupidity or meanness of mules and women, and the heroics of folk heroes such as Big John de Conquer. Janie "thrust herself into the conversation" of the men because they were all in agreement that if Mrs. Tony were married to any of them, they would kill her. Lee Coker comments: "'Ah'd break her or kill her. Makin' uh fool outa me in front of everybody'" (70). "As Janie realizes when she hears this exchange, female obedience and chatteldom are a figurative death" (Sadoff 17). Janie informs the men that "'you don't know half as much 'bout us as you think you do'" out of a growing awareness of her inner self (71). Janie reflects the narrator's ideological stance against the values of the community. These values place the woman in the position of "the mule," always subservient to the male.

Janie's growing awareness of her chatteldom causes her to become less subservient and more resistant to Joe's domination.

As Janie's self-awareness grows, her awareness of Joe's motives also grows. The narrator states: "For the first time she could see a man's head naked of its skull" (73). The tension grows until there is a bitter confrontation. Joe and Janie play the dozens, exchanging mutual insults, and Janie wins. Dianne F. Sadoff states that "Narrative structure implies that Janie's learning to speak out, her willingness to use her tongue as weapon against masculine domination, kills Jody" (17). Certainly, the use of language is presented in terms of power throughout the narrative, so that when Janie tells Joe he has no right to speak of her getting old and then follows it with: "When you pull down yo' britches, you look lak de change uh life." Joe realizes that "Janie had robbed him of his illusion of irresistible maleness that all men cherish, which was terrible" (75).According to Wendy McCredie, Janie actually robs Joe of his authority in the town. "Janie establishes her independence from his voice and causes the death of that voice for the rest of the town. The next time Janie speaks her feelings to Jody, he is on his death bed" (27). As Joe's health declines, Janie learns that both Joe and the community think she has been poisoning him. She also learns that Joe has received treatment from the two-headed doctor, a man characterized by Pheoby as a "multiplied cockroach" (79). It is too late when Janie brings the doctor from Orlando to see him. This doctor diagnoses kidney failure and says he should have been seen two years ago. Joe's death is a major turning point in the novel, an event that enables Janie to act upon her new-found sense of power.

After Joe's death and burial, there is a lengthy psychonarration as Janie takes stock of her mental state. Janie burns her head rags and lets down her hair. She realizes that she has no interest in her long lost mother. "She hated her grandmother and had hidden it from herself all these years under a cloak of pity" (85). She further discovers a "jewel down inside herself" but is prohibited by the community to let it shine. Harriet Jacobs and the African American women who wrote within the confines of the countermyth to the "cult of true womanhood" did not have the freedom to treat parental repudiation in a realistic manner. Hurston is truly revising an earlier tradition. The narrator once again reveals her ideology as Janie resists the community's efforts to find her another man. Janie hears phrases such as "Uh woman by herself is uh pitiful thing" and "you needs uh man" but Janie likes "being lonesome for a change" (86). Janie is in opposition to her community and culture and she approaches the narrator's ideological stance when she tells Pheoby, "Ah jus' loves dis freedom" (89). While Jacobs and other nineteenth century African American women writers spoke of freedom, their use of the word was limited by the confines and structures of their patriarchal communities and society as a whole. Through her use of an "inside view" of Janie, Hurston is challenging and revising the cultural constructs that limited earlier African American women writers.

Janie's lack of dependence on a man for her identity and survival is a threat to her culture's basic beliefs about male-female relationships. She finds herself "glowing inside," however, when she meets a younger man who goes by the name of Tea Cake. For the first time, "somebody wanted her to play" (91). The narrator records the flirting, playful dialogue between Janie and Tea Cake and she also reveals the community's disapproval of Janie's choice. Not only is Tea Cake too young for Janie, but he doesn't "have a dime to cry" (107). The community's opinion matters little to Janie. To Janie, "He was a glance from God" (102). Janie tells Pheoby, "new thoughts had tuh be thought and new words said. After Ah got used tuh dat, we gits 'long jus' fine. He done taught me de maiden language all over" (109). The dialogue between Janie and Tea Cake reveals the equality of their relationship. Melvin Dixon states that

> Hurston's language demonstrates the equality; her sentences balance compound subjects engaged in a single action: 'Tea Cake and Janie gone hunting. Tea Cake and Janie playing checkers; playing coon-can; playing Florida flip on the store porch all afternoon as if nobody else was there'" (89).

The balance of these sentences parallels the equality demonstrated in this phase of the relationship between Janie and Tea Cake. Janie and Tea Cake are indeed engaged in thinking new thoughts and creating a new language that will bridge the communicative chasm that separates male from female.

Janie leaves Eatonville for Jacksonville and there she and Tea Cake are married. They are together only one week when he disappears with her money and all Janie's fears and self-doubts come crashing in upon her. She remembers the story of Annie Tyler who sold her house and went off with a young man only to return to Eatonville alone and destitute.Tea Cake reappears, however, confesses that he is a gambler, and asks Janie's forgiveness. Since the reader has been traveling with Janie during this psychonarration, the reader has some doubts as to Tea Cake's veracity. Janie, on the other hand, after some initial suspicion, seems to accept Tea Cake's story of all-night gambling with a chicken dinner afterward. Since Tea Cake has lost her money, he is determined to win it back. He practices all week, and then takes his dice and disappears once more. For the first time, the narrator reveals Janie's thoughts in free indirect discourse with a merging of the narrator's and Janie's voices. She thinks: "Please, Jesus, don't let them nasty niggers hurt her boy. If they do, Master Jesus, grant her a good gun and a chance to shoot 'em" (120). According to Gates, when free indirect discourse is used "in conjunction with Joe Starks, irony obtains and distancing results; when it is used in conjunction with Janie, empathy obtains and an illusory identification results, an identity we might call lyric fusion between the narrator and Janie" (209). This can be considered a bivocal or double-voiced utterance that is a reflection of Janie's divided self. In fact, there is a mingling of psychonarration and free indirect discourse throughout Janie's coming to terms with herself and her husband. This "lyric fusion" between the narrator and Janie is the structural climax of the novel, because it bridges the communicative chasm between the narrator's and protagonist's voices.

When Tea Cake returns, he gives Janie her money back and they decide to go to the Muck in southern Florida to harvest vegetables and live on the money they make together. The remainder of the narrative concerns their life together on the Muck and the hurricane that forced them to flee for their lives. Tea Cake and Janie are caught in the power of nature and God. The hurricane and resulting flood lead to the event that is to end Tea Cake's life. Tea Cake is bitten by a rabid dog while trying to save Janie. After he contracts rabies, Janie is forced to shoot him. Alice Walker believes that Hurston *permits* Janie to kill Tea Cake in the end because he beats Janie (*Search* 305).

James Krasner believes that Hurston allows Janie's tale to be undercut because "the tale contradicts its own prophetic structure" (118). The story's structure is altered "to transform Tea Cake from perfect husband to a sacrificial victim. His death is both a narrative and a practical necessity. It is the only way to make a clean story out of a messy life so that her prophetic vision can finally be fulfilled" (124). Although Krasner really fails to define exactly what constitutes a "messy" life, he correctly concludes that while Pheoby was Janie's narratee, Janie's story was told for the benefit of the community of Eatonville. Janie realizes that her story will become public knowledge when she says, "mah tongue is in mah friend's mouf" (*Their Eyes* 6). Much as Hurston glossed over many events in her own life, and failed to mention the fulfillment of a life's prophecy she claimed to have seen as a child, both Janie and the public narrator bring *Their Eyes* to somewhat enigmatic closure. Although Janie is at peace with herself and comfortable with the power she has discovered within herself, she, like Jacob's Brent who came before her, remains very much an isolated individual at the close of the narrative.

Susan S. Lanser suggests that a feminist narratology might acknowledge the existence of multiple texts and multiple narratees within a given narrative.[8] Certainly there is a web of embedded narrative texts in *Their Eyes*. The first of these embedded narratives is the quasi-slave narrative told by Nanny. Nanny serves as the narrator of her story and Janie is her narratee. Nanny's story is the only embedded narrative that is told in first person. Nanny tells Janie the story of her escape from slavery and her hopes for her daughter and granddaughter in an effort to make Janie understand why she wants her to marry Logan Killicks. Beyond her immediate reason, however, Nanny's narrative offers an account of black matrilineage and courage that Janie emulates in her resistance to Logan Killicks and Joe Starks. The chatteldom associated with slavery and gender relationships is mirrored in the tales told of Matt Bonner's mule. The mule-talkers are Sam, Lige, and Walter and their narratees are other members of the community. Janie is silenced, but when Joe frees Matt Bonner's mule, she compares his act to Lincoln's Emancipation Proclamation (55). Tea Cake also narrates the story of his adventures with Janie's money to Janie. "Tea Cake stuck out till he had some break-fast, then he talked and acted out the story" (116). Unlike the other narratives, however, Tea Cake's story is told by the public narrator in combination with psychonarration and dialogue. Perhaps this is because it involves either a rejection or the deception of Janie. At any rate, it serves to distance Tea Cake from his tale, and makes it seem less reliable than other embedded narratives. All these narratives serve as a comment on gender relationships in one way or another. Nanny's narrative is the shared communication that takes place between women, the narratives of the porch talkers represent less personal, more male-oriented folk tales, and Tea Cake's narrative reveals the emotional gulf that often distances men from women. The use of embedded narratives reflects Jacobs's slave narrative. Hurston's use of embedded narratives differs from Jacobs's, because Hurston uses them to comment on gender relationships rather than slave-master relationships.

In addition to multiple narratives within the textual framework of *Their Eyes Were Watching God*, there are multiple implied readers. Barbara Johnson states that she had a lot to learn, "from Hurston's way of dealing with multiple agendas and heterogeneous implied readers" (278). Although Johnson is writing in reference to two of Hurston's essays, her statement may be applied to *Their Eyes*. Hurston's novel was undoubtedly written to sell to an Anglo as well as an African American audience, and to appeal to men as well as women. According to Holt, "one of the primary functions of black autobiography is to unify the writer and his readers around the common core of experience that they share" (36). The autobiographical aspect of *Their Eyes* leads the reader to conclude that the implied readers of the text are certainly African Americans. By studying the voices within the text, however, one may conclude that the "subversive" message within the text was addressed primarily to African American women. Because she addresses her narrative to African American women, Hurston's text can be considered a major revision of nineteenth century African American women's writing.

There are several important links between the authorial voice and public narrator's. First, they share the same ideological stance. Both voices advocate freedom from sexist and racist oppression, and both represent a rejection of community and cultural values that enforce such oppression. These voices also share an imaginative consciousness that speaks of wandering, far horizon, and independence in a time when women were somewhat restricted. Janie goes to the gate to look down the road much as Hurston did as a young girl. "My favorite place was atop the gate-post" (*I Love* 152). The ideological stance and imaginative consciousness are revealed somewhat carefully. Janie is passive and meek in the opening chapters. The reader is more than one-third of the way through the text before Janie tells the men, "It's so easy to make yo'self out God Almighty when you ain't got nothin' to strain against but women and chickens" (71). Janie's dialect is also a link between the authorial and narrative voices. Janie's speech is a part of her identity and represents the speech forms that Zora Neale Hurston heard as a child growing up in Florida. The very movement from educated standard language into dialect and back again is symbolic of the bond between the narrative and authorial voices. One of the most remarkable aspects of *Their Eyes* is the bridging of authorial and narrative voices.

Janie does not tell her story in her own voice; her voice is intrinsically linked to the public narrator's. What some critics perceive as her lack of voice has been a subject of debate for years. Jennifer Jordan believes that *Their Eyes* fails as a feminist document because Janie never perceives herself as an independent, intrinsically fulfilled human being. Nor does she form the strong female and racial bonds that black feminists have deemed necessary in their definition of an ideologically correct literature (115). Most critics and many black feminist critics certainly do not agree with Jordan. W. Lawrence Hogue states that "As a literary discourse, feminism informs Hurston's *Their Eyes Were Watching God*" (59). This text contains images such as the domineering patriarch and the somewhat battered Janie that have been essential to past feminist ideology. Moreover, it negates the traditional subject-object dichotomy associated with gender by transforming Janie into a speaking subject. Despite the somewhat enigmatic close of *Their Eyes*, Janie emerges as an independent, self-aware individual. This narrative traces the movement of Janie from object to subject, from a passive woman with no voice who is dominated by her husband to a woman who can think and act for herself. According to Hortense J. Spillers, "Janie Starks becomes the individual-

ized subject of her own experience" (253). It is the acquisition
of voice and consciousness that enables Janie to act as an agent
who can "*make* her world, just as she is *made* by it" (Spillers
255). This preoccupation with language is more than evident
in *Their Eyes*. The numerous references to language include
many already mentioned; Joe's "big voice," Janie's "new words"
and "new language," Tea Cake's "maiden language" to name a
few. Hurston also calls attention to the different patterns of
speech and thought found in men and women. Hurston's narrative implies "that gender may be a greater source of oppression and repression than is ethnicity" (Kitch 68). In fact, Rita
Terezinha Schmidt considers "the exploration of male/female
power relations" the central core of Hurston's fiction (3). Other
critics would argue that gender only seems to be a greater
source of oppression because Hurston, to some extent, limited the scope of the narrative to the African American community itself.

The circular structure of this text is reflected in Janie's voice;
as it geographically moves Janie from Eatonville and brings
her back, it also brings her into relation with her voice as it
exists at the beginning of the text. Unlike Harriet Jacobs who
is unable to return to her community of origin, Janie comes
back to Eatonville a new woman. The voices of the narrator,
the protagonist and the author are also linked in such a manner. According to hooks, "Third person narration calls attention to Hurston's authorial voice, highlighting the importance
of writing" ("Zora" 11). Just as the narrative voice moves toward convergence with Janie's voice, the formal voice of the
public narrator is closely associated with the text's authorial
voice. "Third-person narrators, who are telling a story in which
they themselves do not participate as characters, are far more
likely than first-person narrator-characters to present an equivalence with the authorial voice" (Lanser *Narrative Act* 152). Robert B. Stepto certainly agrees with this analysis regarding *Their
Eyes*. He states: "On one hand, third-person narration of Janie's
tale helps to build a space (or at least the illusion of space)
between author and character, for the author and her audience alike; on the other, when told in this fashion control of
the tale remains, no matter how unintended, with the author
alone" (166). The distancing, then, of this narrator simply

serves to bring her voice into a closer relationship with the author's. The author's, narrator's, and protagonist's voices, then, are so closely interconnected that the reader may at times have difficulty accurately distinguishing between the three of them. Paradoxically, Hurston's voice stands in closer relation to her third-person narrative than Jacobs's voice stands in relation to her first-person narrative.

The syntax, lexis, and morphology of *Their Eyes* is very like that in *Dust Tracks on a Road* and *Mules and Men*. "In other words, the equivalence of author and narrator implies an authorial responsibility that is similar to an author's responsibility for his or her nonfictional work" (Lanser *Narrative Act* 153). While this narrator can be linked to the authorial voice, she can also "move in and out of various relationships to the author" (150). Both the authorial and narrative voice make use of anthropology to move the story forward. In fact, one can often see a double discourse of narrative and authorial voice in *Their Eyes* that is mirrored to some extent in the free indirect discourse that moves the narrator into close proximity to Janie's voice similar to Janie's division into "inside and outside." The reader can hear a dual discourse within this relationship of voice; the narrative voice that propels Janie toward self-knowledge, and the authorial voice that speaks from Hurston's background and education as an anthropologist. Both of these voices remain within the African American autobiographical genre. Stephen Butterfield defines the period in which Hurston wrote as the second phase of African American autobiography, a phase that lasted roughly from 1901 to 1961, as a phase in which authors searched for a unified self. During this phase the autobiographies "are more literary and introspective, the styles are sharply individualized, and the identity more alienated, not only from white America, but from other blacks" (Butterfield 7).[9] The search for self is the ultimate quest not only for Harriet Jacobs, but also for both Janie and Hurston, a quest that causes Hurston's "official," as well as her unofficial, autobiographical writings to be focused on the individual, to remain descriptive, and to fail to propose new paradigms for society.

Chapter Three

Alice Walker's
The Color Purple

Zora Neale Hurston and Harriet Jacobs can be considered public poets because they identify at least a portion of their narratives as autobiographical and address them to the reading public. Alice Walker, on the other hand, is what Richard Hugo terms a "private" poet.[1]

Readers cannot hear the autobiographical voice in Walker's *The Color Purple* (1982) as easily as they hear the voice in Hurston's *Dust Tracks on a Road* and *Their Eyes Were Watching God* or Jacobs's *Incidents in the Life of a Slave Girl*. On the other hand, Walker has written extensively about her characters, their lives, and the act of creating them. Because she has written about her life, her opinions, and her writing, the authorial voice is identifiable in *The Color Purple*. Walker herself says that she allows her characters "to *speak* through me" (*Search* 356). Walker explains that she was forced to leave New York while writing *The Color Purple* because her characters were constantly complaining about the city. She tried to write in San Francisco, but was finally forced to move to northern California to a place that "looked a lot like the town in Georgia most of them were from, only it was more beautiful and the local swimming hole was not segregated" (*Search* 357).

Like Jacobs's Edenton, North Carolina and Hurston's Eatonville, Florida the setting for Walker's novel is near Eatonton, Georgia, the rural area where she was raised. Walker, in a manner similar to Hurston's, draws the imagery, characterizations and language for her novel from her childhood

home. Walker's parents worked as sharecroppers in rural Georgia and family and friends serve as starting points for many of
her narratives. She describes how she discovered the germ of
the story that became *The Color Purple*:

> I was hiking through the woods with my sister, Ruth, talking about a
> lovers' triangle of which we both knew. She said: 'And you know, one
> day The Wife asked The Other Woman for a pair of her drawers.'
> Instantly the missing piece of the story I was mentally writing—about
> two women who felt married to the same man—fell into place (*Search*
> 355).

Walker's novel grew, then, from this family story. It diverged
from this "germ" of her story and incorporated other stories
and personalities, but throughout *The Color Purple* the reader
can discern the authorial voice.

One way the reader can locate Walker's authorial voice in
The Color Purple is by identifying her obsessions. Walker is obviously committed to exposing the oppression of black women.
As she writes, "I am committed to exploring the oppressions,
the insanities, the loyalties, and the triumphs of black women
(*Search* 251). Walker's voice explores women's roles within the
patriarchal system, emphasizing their desires for freedom, spirituality and creativity. According to Mary Helen Washington,
Walker is especially preoccupied with the subject of the psy-
chic and physical oppression of women. Washington writes of
an interview with Walker: "Ms. Walker spoke of her own awareness of and experiences with brutality and violence in the lives
of black women, many of whom she had known as a girl growing up in Eatonton, Georgia, some in her own family" (Washington, "Essay" 134).

In a later publication, Walker discusses the impact of patriarchal violence within her own family. When she was seven
years old, her brother shot her in the eye with an air rifle, and
the copper pellet used in the rifle destroyed the pupil of her
eye. For many years afterward, Walker considered herself disfigured and devalued. Walker's parents, who bought guns for
their sons, referred to the event as "Alice's accident," but as an
adult, Walker describes her blinding as a "patriarchal wound"
(*Warrior Marks* 17). Celie, the protagonist of *The Color Purple*,
is psychically and sexually abused by the man she believes is

her father. Celie states: "He never have a kine word to say to me. Just say You gonna do what your mammy wouldn't" (*Color* 1). After giving birth to two children by this man, Celie is traded like chattel to the man she calls "Mister." When Celie is summoned by her "Pa," her future husband, who has accepted the cow and linens that come with her, "look me up and down" (*Color* 11). Harriet Jacobs recounts a similar image in *Incidents* when Dr. Flint decided to sell her grandmother, Aunt Marthy. "When the day of sale came, she took her place among the chattels, and at the first call she sprang upon the auction-block" (11). Both Celie and Aunt Marthy are victims of a patriarchal system that reduces them to the status of property.

Walker focuses on the issue of the powerlessness of Southern black women throughout her novels, short stories and essays. Within the patriarchal system, women are objectified and often regarded as less than human. In *The Color Purple*, Sofia complains that all Harpo wants is obedience from her. "He don't want a wife, he want a dog" (*Color* 68). In Walker's short story "Roselily" the protagonist finds herself in the midst of a wedding ceremony in which she is being married to a Black Muslim. Like Celie she has little choice in the matter and feels "something . . . behind her eyes. She thinks of the something as a rat trapped, cornered, scurrying to and fro in her head, peering through the windows of her eyes" (*In Love* 8). Many of the women in Walker's stories feel helpless and trapped by either husbands or fathers, or both. The images of entrapment and powerlessness are also very much a part of the narratives of Harriet Jacobs and Zora Neale Hurston.

The powerlessness Walker's women feel is often reaffirmed by the physical abuse they endure in their marriages. Many of the women in Walker's stories have been silenced by abuse. According to Belenky and others, "The actions of these women are in the form of unquestioned submission to the immediate commands of authorities" (28). When Celie's stepfather tells her to "never tell nobody but God" after he has raped and abused her, Celie obeys by writing her story in a series of letters to God. When her husband beats her, Celie survives by refusing to feel. "I make myself wood" (*Color* 23). Mem Copeland, in *The Third Life of Grange Copeland* is another of Walker's powerless, silent women. She endures "many years of

Saturday-night beatings" and although she makes an attempt to better her condition and that of her children, she is permanently silenced by her shotgun-wielding husband (*Third* 130). The imagery for this murder came from an experience Walker had as a child. According to Washington, "a friend's father killed his wife, and Walker, a curious child, saw the mother's body laid out on a slab in the funeral home." The image of this body stayed with Walker. As an adult she remembered the woman "lying on the slab with half her head shot off, and on her feet were those shoes that I describe—hole in the bottom, and she had stuffed paper in them" (Washington, "Essay" 136). This very imagery is used to describe Mem Copeland's body as it lay on the walk outside her house.

Violence directed toward women is prefigured in earlier texts by African American women. Harriet Jacobs is not only beaten by her master but is also threatened by "death, and worse than death" (32). Hurston's protagonist, Janie, is beaten by all three of her husbands, and Hurston herself admits that her husband, A. W. Price, used physical violence against her (*Dust Tracks* 186). Physical violence is a real presence in all of the narratives under consideration, but only in *The Color Purple*, as Celie stands over Mr._____ with a razor in her hand, does the author confront her own potential for violence and transcends it (Tusmith 72).

In *The Color Purple*, Mister's first wife, Annie Julia, is subjected to insult and injury by both Mister and his lover, Shug. Annie Julia takes a lover who also abuses her and finally kills her in front of her son, Harpo. Harpo cradles his dying mother's head in his arms. Walker undoubtedly drew from family stories as she created the murder of Annie Julia and its effect upon Harpo. In her essay entitled "Father," Walker describes her father's childhood. "His mother had been murdered, by a man who claimed to love her, when he was eleven. His father, to put it very politely, drank and terrorized his children" (*Living* 14). In Walker's short story, "The Child Who Favored Daughter," the father cuts off his daughter's breasts because she is dating a white boy. The daughter is silenced by her father, a man whose soul is so disfigured by racism that he cannot endure a disobedient daughter who has become a "'white man's slut'" (*In Love* 41). Walker states in an interview that she has always wanted to explore relationships between men and women to know why "women are always condemned for doing what men do as an expression of their masculinity" (*Search* 156). The powerlessness of women is only a part of Walker's concern with familial relations.

At the heart of these relations, and related to women's lack of power, is Walker's concern with the overall effects of sexism. After describing how her father "expected his sons to have sex with women," Walker says she "was relieved to know his sexist behavior was not something uniquely his own, but, rather, an imitation of the behavior of the society around us" (*Search* 330). Sexist behavior on the part of men is a recurring image in Walker's novels. In *The Third Life of Grange Copeland* Brownfield tells Mem that nobody will hire her because she is "'a snaggle-toothed old *plow* mule.'" He tells her to "'look in the glass sometime. You ain't just ugly and beat-up looking, you's old!'" (124). Societal attitudes in the United States cause both men and women to focus on women's bodies and outward appearance.

Walker's concern for women is global. In *The Color Purple*, Nettie, Celie's sister, discovers that the Olinka people of Africa think very little of women who are not connected to men through marriage. In this society women have status only as mothers. When Nettie states that she is not the mother of anybody's children but is still something, she is told: "'You are not much'" (162). Walker expands her concern for African women in her novel, *Possessing the Secret of Joy* and in her documentary film and publication, *Warrior Marks*. In *Possessing the Secret of Joy*, Walker tackles the issue of female circumcision, which she calls the "sexual blinding" of women. Her protagonist, Evelyn Johnson, explains that she had herself circumcised in order "to be accepted as a real woman" by the Olinka people and that no man "would even think of marrying a woman who was not circumcised" (122). Walker has devoted her most recent years to fighting for women throughout the world, for those "survivors and champions" who refuse to become victims of sexist traditions (*Warrior Marks* 204).

In *The Color Purple*, when Sofia's mother dies, Harpo argues that she and her sisters should not be pall bearers. "Women weaker, he say. People think they weaker, say they weaker, anyhow. Women spose to take it easy. Cry if you want to. Not try to take over" (225). Of course, Mister makes what is perhaps the most sexist statement in *The Color Purple*. When Shug announces that Celie is going to Memphis with her, Mister tells Celie that she is worthless. "You black, you pore, you ugly, you a woman. Goddam, he say, you nothing at all" (213). Walker explains why she is so concerned with such sexism in her essay entitled "Looking to the Side, and Back." "It was at the Radcliffe symposium that I saw that black women are more loyal to black men than they are to themselves, a dangerous state of affairs that has its logical end in self-destruction" (*Search* 318). Walker advocates a sisterhood of black women, really all women, who will support each other in resisting patriarchy.

The patriarchal system objectifies women. Since many of Walker's short stories and novels are women-centered or womanist, she often focuses on the objectification of women. Many of her heroines either become or are introduced to the reader as active, speaking subjects. Celie is introduced as a woman who first writes, and then speaks herself into existence. Through her letters she moves from oral silence to speaking subject, or as she says "into creation." She announces: "I'm pore, I'm black, I may be ugly and can't cook. . . But I'm here" (*Color* 214). In her short story "Coming Apart," Walker confronts the issue of pornography and the objectification of black women. The husband, who has been addicted to pornographic photos, realizes, through the active insistence of his mate, that he thinks of his wife as "*still* black, whereas he feels himself to have moved to some other plane" (*Can't* 48). This man sees women as objects and himself as the subject. His objectification of women extends to his wife. This husband, much as Mister in *The Color Purple*, realizes that "to make love to his wife as she really is, as who she really is—indeed, to make love to any other human being as they really are—will require a soul-rending look into himself" (*Can't* 51).

Susanne Kappeler contends that the subject-object dichotomy, the root of pornography, prevents effective communication between men and women.[2] "He is a pure subject in relation to an object, which means that he is not engaging in exchange or communication with that objectified person, who by definition, cannot take the role of a subject" (61). She identifies the oppression of white women and the "double oppression" of black women as cultural constructs, a "convenient excuse for the establishment of oppressive social systems" (217). In a similar manner, Walker concludes that "the more ancient roots of modern pornography are to be found in the almost always pornographic treatment of black women, who, from the moment they entered slavery, even in their own homelands, were subjected to rape as the 'logical' convergence of sex and violence. Conquest, in short" (*Can't* 42). Harriet Jacobs's narrative gives testimony to the sexual assaults experienced by slave women, and adds historical validity to Walker's statement. Conquest, oppression and accompanying violence toward objectified humans are the historical accomplishments of the individualized subject.

The patriarchal system itself enslaves and degrades women, for it institutionalizes and valorizes the subject-object dichotomy. Woman, according to Simone de Beauvoir, "is defined and differentiated with reference to man and not he with reference to her; she is the incidental, the inessential as opposed to the essential. He is the Subject, he is the Absolute—she is the Other" (xvi). In *The Color Purple*, Celie, with Shug's help, succeeds in freeing herself, (de)objectifying herself, from this system which is characterized by interlocking dualisms. The women in this novel form a community that resists patriarchal control. According to Bettye Parker-Smith, "They are sisters in body as well as in spirit and the spirit *cannot* be broken" (485). Walker is not advocating the destruction of men themselves, but of a system that robs both men and women of their humanity. According to Barbara Christian, Walker "sees the possibility of empowerment for black women if they create a community of sisters that can alter the present-day unnatural definitions of woman and man" (*Black Feminist* 181). At the end of *The Color Purple*, Celie and Mister actually become rather close friends. Because of her love for Shug, Celie is able to move toward an understanding of the man she only knew as "Mister" for many years.

Walker describes the patriarchal system as "the enemy within . . . that has kept women virtual slaves throughout memory" (*Search* 379). She actually moves beyond the restoration of Celie's voice to approve the destruction of "the patriarchal marriage plot that sanctions violence against women" (Froula 639). In *The Temple of My Familiar*, Walker openly prescribes the abolition of such marriage. The protagonist, Suwelo, explains why he and Fanny decided to divorce. Couples, though living together, often individuate and eventually separate from each other. "There is no longer a spiritual or even an authentic physical connection. Instead, they are connected by house payments, a car, children, political expediency, whatever. The divorce was merely our first shedding of any nonintrinsic relatedness." While Fanny believed that marriage did not fit anyone, Suwelo was not so sure, "being a man within a patriarchal system" (*Temple* 282). Fanny is connected to *The Color Purple*. She is Olivia's daughter, and remembers fondly the relationship between Shug and her grandmother, Celie. She is another expression of the resistance to the patriarchal system presented in *The Color Purple*. A recurring motif within almost all of Walker's texts is identified by Rafe in *The Temple of My Familiar*: "Ruling over other people automatically cuts you off from life" (368). Walker advocates alternative relationships for men and women, situations in which women do not see themselves solely in relation to black men. The men and women in both *The Color Purple* and *The Temple of My Familiar* make significant progress toward intersubjectivity, where neither is objectified and both are free to express themselves as creative subjects. Walker signifies upon Hurston's texts as she moves her protagonists into intersubjective relationships. Although Janie and Tea Cake initially move toward intersubjectivity in *Their Eyes Were Watching God*, they are ultimately unable to resolve the conflicts within their relationship.

Walker advocates freedom of expression for women. In her essay "In the Closet of the Soul," she argues for sexual freedom. "Women loving women, and expressing it 'publicly,' if they so choose, is part and parcel of what freedom for women means, just as this is what it means for anyone else." Walker believes that a person who is not free to express his or her love is enslaved, just as anyone who would prohibit expression of love has a "slaveholder's mentality" (*Living* 91). When Celie is beaten by her stepfather because he says she has winked at a boy, she writes: "I don't even look at mens. That's the truth. I look at women, tho, cause I'm not scared of them" (*Color* 6).

Celie is attracted to Shug. "First time I got the full sight of Shug Avery, I thought I had turned into a man" (51). The two women live together for awhile until Shug meets a young man and falls in love with him. Celie is heartbroken and returns home. During this period of her life Celie and Mister become friends and he proposes marriage "in the spirit as well as in the flesh." Celie, however, is not attracted to men, they are all "frogs" to her. She also allows Shug to follow her own feelings. "Just cause I love her don't take away none of her rights" (*Color* 276).

According to Barbara Christian, "Walker in *The Color Purple* does for the sexual relationships between black women what Hurston in *Their Eyes Were Watching God* did for sexual relationships between black women and men" (*Black Feminist* 184). While Jacobs, as a slave woman, is unable to portray intersubjective sexual relationships, both Hurston and Walker create female subjects who assert their sexual and emotional independence. In her essay "Breaking Chains and Encouraging Life," Walker encourages black women writers and nonwriters to affirm the rights of black lesbian women by declaring, "*We are all lesbians*" (*Search* 289). Adrienne Rich describes the power of women in similar terms. She states:

> I believe it is the lesbian in every woman who is compelled by female energy, who gravitates toward strong women, who seeks a literature that will express that energy and strength. It is the lesbian in us who drives us to feel imaginatively, render in language, grasp, the full connection between woman and woman" (200).

The love between Shug and Celie is intersubjective because both women are free to love and each is a speaking subject. Walker brings the two women back together in *The Temple of My Familiar* as they live out their lives together in the house that Celie inherited from her father. And, Walker, who describes herself as a "homospiritual" would probably agree with Rich that primarily women-oriented women are, in a larger sense, lesbians (*Living* 163).

Walker calls these woman-oriented women, "womanists" rather than feminists.[3] Some of these women are heterosexual, such as the protagonist of the short story, "Coming Apart," who thinks of herself as a womanist (*Can't* 41-53). Walker states:

"A womanist is a feminist, only more common. (The author of this piece is a womanist)" (*Can't* 48). Walker defends black women who love other women, because she believes they also "have concern, in a culture that oppresses all black people (and this would go back very far), for their fathers, brothers, and sons, no matter how they feel about them as males." Walker often portrays such women as living apart from men. In *The Color Purple*, Celie and Shug live apart from men for awhile, and at the end, Celie chooses to live in her own house. In *The Temple of My Familiar*, Miss Lizzie tells Suwelo about the peaceful foundation of her many lives. She remembers the very small people she lived with, where "the children live with the mothers and the aunts; our fathers and uncles are nearby, and we visit and are visited by them, but we live with the women" (*Temple* 84). Such sex-segregated living arrangements have historic precedents in seventeenth- and eighteenth-century West African traditions. As Deborah Gray White writes, "West African women usually did not raise small children with the help of their husbands, but raised them alone or with the assistance of other women" (65).[1]

In *The Color Purple* Mister tells Celie that he loves Shug because she is so honest and upright. "Shug act more manly than most men." Celie on the other hand, thinks not. "What Shug got is womanly it seem like to me" (276). Walker warns black women not to "dissociate themselves from the women's movement," for fear of abandoning "their responsibilities to women throughout the world" (*Search* 379). Walker's womanly, "womanist," authorial voice advocates healing wounds and opening communication between men and women within the African American community. Zora Neale Hurston earlier proposed bridging the communication chasm between African American men and women in her discourse between Janie and Tea Cake. Walker forcefully reiterates Hurston's proposal throughout her novels and short stories.

The themes of forgiveness and reconciliation are prominent in Walker's writing. In *The Temple of My Familiar* Walker's character-actors work toward forgiveness of each other. Fanny writes to Suwelo: "Forgiveness is the true foundation of health and happiness, just as it is for any lasting progress. Without forgiveness there is no forgetfulness of evil; without forgetfulness there still remains the threat of violence" (308). In *The Color Purple*, Celie forgives Mister. She realizes that she no longer hates him. She cannot hate him because he loves Shug and because "look like he trying to make something out of himself. I mean when you talk to him now he really listen" (267).

While Walker affirms her belief in intersubjective relationships for men and women, her attitude toward women's bodies and pregnancy is somewhat ambivalent. According to Sabine Bröck and Anne Konen, "In Walker's underlying concept of sexuality . . . the female body is regarded as woman's enemy, a trap; a girl's first menstruation is consequently described as an initiation into the terrors of patriarchal society" (172). Many of the images of women's bodies and sexuality in Walker's novels and short stories are presented in less than positive terms. In *The Color Purple* pregnancy is presented as a trap. Celie worries that her stepfather will sexually abuse her sister Nettie, so she urges her to marry Mister. "I say Marry him, Nettie, and try to have one good year out your life. After that, I know she be big" (6). Pregnancy ends Celie's dreams for independence; she can only hope that her sister can escape through education. In the first years of the twentieth century, many African Americans hoped that education would bring them independence. While obtaining a higher education was difficult for men, many African American women found the pursuit of education almost impossible. "Speeches and articles abound citing black women as the nurturers and the guardians of—not the thinkers or leaders of the race" (Perkins 24). Women's dreams were certainly limited by the demands of motherhood. Similarly, In *The Third Life of Grange Copeland* Mem is brought back to "lowness" through the "weakness" of her womb. "The two pregnancies he forced on her in the new house, although they did not bear live fruit, almost completely destroyed what was left of her health" (147).

Walker's attitude toward women's bodies and pregnancy is prefigured by both Hurston and Jacobs. Zora Neale Hurston's protagonist, Janie, is also entrapped by her sexuality. When her grandmother realizes that Janie has reached adolescence, she marries her to Logan Killicks. Janie's mother, like Mem Copeland, is brought to "lowness" through the "weakness" of her womb. Leafy is raped by her teacher, and her life falls

apart after the birth of Janie (*Their Eyes* 8-19). Harriet Jacobs
takes a white lover as a grand show of choice, but the two children that are produced from their relationship not only anger
her master, Dr. Flint, but also keep Jacobs in Edenton, trapped
in the garret of her grandmother's house (*Incidents* 114-117).

Walker's images of entrapment not only reflect an obsession of many African American women but also may well be
autobiographical. Walker explores the alternative to pregnancy
in her short story "The Abortion." Her protagonist agonizes
that she is "Still not in control of her sensuality, and only
through violence and with money (for the flight, for the op-
eration itself) in control of her body" (*Can't* 69). As a young
woman, Walker returned to complete her last year of college
after a summer in Africa "healthy and brown" and pregnant.
She states that she "felt at the mercy of everything, including
my own body." After coping with an abortion on her own she
states that she "began to understand how alone woman is, because of her body" (*Search* 248). In her essay "One Child of
One's Own," Walker discusses the conflict that many artists
and writers face when contemplating parenthood. She states:
"For me, there has been conflict, struggle, occasional defeat—
not only in affirming the life of my own child (children) at all
costs, but also in seeing in that affirmation a fond acceptance
and confirmation of myself in a world that would deny me the
untrampled blossoming of my own existence" (*Search* 362).
Because of her need to write, to create, she made the decision
to have only one child. "`With more than one you're a sitting
duck'" (*Search* 363). Walker is passionately committed to the
blossoming of the lives of women.

Despite Walker's ambivalent attitude toward women's bodies and sexuality, she is a committed mother. The joys and
trials of motherhood, especially for the African American
woman, is an ever present part of her writing. In her essay on
"Writing the Color Purple," she discusses her feelings when
she learned that her daughter would be living with her for two
years: "Could I handle it?" She discovered that not only could
she handle it, but "My characters adored her" (*Search* 359).
The Color Purple opens with the birth of Celie's second child.
Both her children are taken from her, but she thinks of herself
as their mother, and is finally reunited with them at the end of

the novel. Meridian, the protagonist of the novel *Meridian*, gives her child up for adoption in order to receive a scholarship that will enable her to attend college. Meridian is haunted by the guilt that she feels regarding this child. Shug, in *The Color Purple* also gives up her children; this time to her parents to raise. Shug, like Meridian feels guilty because she has given up her children, but later is reconciled with at least one of them.

The importance of motherhood and modeling within the African American community is further demonstrated in Walker's search for what she terms a literary "foremother." She finds this foremother in Zora Neale Hurston and describes her search in her essays "In Search of Our Mother's Gardens" and "Looking for Zora." In her essays on Hurston, Walker describes how she first heard the names of now famous black women writers "appended, like verbal footnotes, to the illustrious all-male list that paralleled them" (*Search* 84). She relates her need for a literary foremother and explains how her discovery of Hurston fulfilled that need. Walker states that were she condemned to a desert island for life, she would take with her Hurston's *Mules and Men* and *Their Eyes Were Watching God*. Of *Their Eyes* she emphatically states: "*There is no book more important to me than this one*" (*Search* 86). According to Molly Hite, both Walker and Hurston turn their attention to conventionally marginal protagonists in order to let those characters assert their voices "in a world full of speechmakers" (267). Hurston and Walker create women who unexpectedly transform themselves from objects into speaking subjects within the African American community. These creations of Walker and Hurston emerge from their narratives as independent, empowered beings who take charge of their own lives. Walker describes how she traveled to Florida, representing herself as Hurston's niece in order to gain information about her and locate her grave (*Search* 93-116). Hite argues that Walker recreates her relationship with Hurston "as a reciprocal and interactive one," and that Walker "dramatizes Hurston's literary role as the undoer of inessential and divisive hierarchies" by casting Hurston in the role of Shug in *The Color Purple* (273).

While Walker emphasizes the intersection of racism and sexism throughout her writings, her focus, like Hurston's, is on relationships within the African American community. In an interview with Claudia Tate, Walker states: "Twentieth-century black women writers all seem to be much more interested in the black community, in intimate relationships, with the white world as a *backdrop*, which is certainly the appropriate perspective, in my view" (Walker, Interview 181). The white community exists on the fringes of consciousness in Walker's characters much as it does in Hurston's characters, but its oppression, the oppression expressed through patriarchy, reaches into the black community. Both Walker and Hurston explore the indirect effects that racism has on their protagonists.

In Hurston's *Their Eyes Were Watching God*, Mis' Turner, a light-skinned African American states emphatically that she cannot understand why Janie is married to dark-skinned Tea Cake. "'Ah jus' couldn't see mahself married to no black man. It's too many black folks already. We oughta lighten up de race'" (134). In *The Color Purple*, Sofia is sent to prison for slugging the white mayor of the town. She is beaten and abused and her spirit is broken. She tells Celie that in order to survive, "Every time they ast me to do something, Miss Celie, I act like I'm you. I jump right up and do just what they say" (93). This is a mirror image of the relationship Celie has with Mister, an image that folds back in upon itself in the patriarchal system. Walker brings the system full circle in *The Color Purple* when Celie tells "Mr. _____" what Nettie wrote to her about the Olinka people. It seems that the Olinka's historical knowledge extended to the time beyond the Biblical Adam; therefore, they explained to Nettie that Adam was not the first man, that white people had been born to the Olinka peoples and "they throwed out the white Olinka peoples for how they look. They want everybody to be just alike" (*Color* 280). The essence of patriarchy in all cultures seems to be the need to assign status based on difference.

In Eurocentric cultures, those who are different, those who are seen as the Other, are dark-skinned people. In *The Third Life of Grange Copeland*, Brownfield wonders at the white man who is able to "turn his father into something that might as well have been a pebble or a post or a piece of dirt, but after he becomes a victim of racism himself, he reproaches his wife with her color. "He liked to sling the perfection of white women at her because color was something she could not change and as his own colored skin annoyed him he meant for hers to humble her" (*Color* 84). Brownfield is passing on to his wife the oppression and abuse that white society has exerted on him and his father before him. The reader can see most clearly in this novel the guilt that black women often feel for the emasculation of black men. "Black women not only digest the hurt and pain, they feel it their duty to become a repository of the Black man's rage" (Parker-Smith 481). In *The Color Purple* the author offers an alternative. Celie, Harpo, Mary Agnes, Mister and Shug realize they must get Sofia out of jail, that she will die if she remains in prison. They plot together, Mary Agnes agrees to seduce the jailer, and they successfully manipulate the racist system that threatens Sofia's life. Throughout *The Color Purple*, the authorial voice speaks for subverting a system that promotes both racism and sexism.

Walker does encourage black men and women to support each other, and she disparages the incipient racism so often found within the African American community itself, especially the significance attached to skin color. There are numerous references to skin color in *The Color Purple*. Harpo tells Celie that Sofia is "bright." Celie asks him if he means "smart," and he replies "Naw. Bright *skin*. She smart too though, I think" (31). Obviously, the color of Sofia's skin is more important to Harpo than her intelligence. Mister's father comes to visit when he hears that Shug is staying at his son' house. He proceeds to insult Shug by telling his son that "she black as tar, she nappy headed." (*Color* 56). Finally, Nettie tells Celie that Tashi has real misgivings about leaving Africa for America. Tashi has read magazines from the United States and "it was very clear to her that black people did not truly admire blackskinned black people like herself, and especially did not admire blackskinned black women" (*Color* 286). Walker responds to novels of the nineteenth century that portray African American protagonists with fair skin. She argues that, "black men could be depicted as literally black and still be considered men (since dark *is* masculine to the Euro-American mind), the blackskinned woman, being dark and female, must perforce be whitened, since 'fairness' was and is the standard of Euro-American femininity" (*Search* 301). Walker believes that the fair-skinned African Americans will disappear as blacks, that they will "pass" into white America with little connection to their heritage. She calls for attention to this situation, for "it is the whole family, rather than the dark or the light, that must be affirmed. Light-and white-skinned black women will lose their only link to rebellion against white America if they cut themselves off from the black woman" (*Search* 311).

Walker recalls her father's "colorism." "He *did* fall in love with my mother partly because she was so light; he never denied it" (*Search* 330). Walker's women are often dark-skinned African Americans, and they are direct links to the community of their heritage. Walker states: "What the black Southern writer inherits as a natural right is a sense of *community*" (*Search* 17). Both Walker and the women she creates advocate a removal of the hypocrisy that preaches "Black is Beautiful" while operating within a Eurocentric patriarchy that, while objectifying women, sets its own standards of beauty. Both Harriet Jacobs and Hurston's Janie Woods are light-skinned women with European features, women whose appearance makes them more acceptable within their respective communities. Walker revises their images of beauty as well as the writing of other African American women who glorify the light-skinned mulatta as a part of the countermyth.

Walker is obsessed with spirituality, her own as well as her characters. Celie writes her letters to God because she is too ashamed to speak aloud what has happened to her. During her life with Mister, she consoles herself with thoughts such as "This life soon be over. Heaven last all ways" (*Color* 44). Once she gains her voice, however, her image of God begins to change. Shug assures her that God loves sex, and that God is not white but is in everything. Walker states that she is "constantly involved, internally, with religious questions, that she does not believe in God, but sees God in nature. "The world is God. Man is God. So is a leaf or a snake. . ." (*Search* 264). Celie expresses this view of God as she addresses her last letter. "Dear God. Dear stars, dear trees, dear sky, dear peoples. Dear Everything. Dear God" (*Color* 292). The authorial voice is perhaps most evident in *The Color Purple* when Shug states: "I think it pisses God off if you walk by the color purple in a field somewhere and don't notice it" (203). Although Shug refuses to be bound down, according to Catherine Keller, "she does not give up on religion as attunement to the interconnected whole of things." Shug, with her female sense of being part of everything, tells Celie: "One day when I was sitting quiet and feeling like a motherless chile, which I was, it come to me: that feeling of being part of everything, not separate at all. I knew that if I cut a tree, my arm would bleed" (203). According to Keller, this is a clear case of "oceanic feeling," of feeling connected to all of life, to all of creation.[5] The connectivity of women is an underlying theme in both *The Color Purple* and *The Temple of My Familiar*. Celie's connection to the whole of things is prefigured in Hurston's *Their Eyes Were Watching God*. When the wind that accompanies the hurricane threatens destruction,

> Janie and Tea Cake sat in company with the others in other shanties, their eyes straining against crude walls and their souls asking if He meant to measure their puny might against His. They seemed to be staring at the dark, but their eyes were watching God (151).

This view of God and religion is expanded in *The Temple of My Familiar*. Olivia tells Fanny that her father Samuel eventually ceased believing in Christianity because he saw it "as a religion of conquest and domination inflicted on other peoples" (146). In this sequel to *The Color Purple* Celie and Shug form a religious community they call a "band," and Rafe remembers "that women were called *first* and this calling was something men took away from them" (98). Shug even writes her own beatitudes or "helps" produced as "The Gospel According to Shug" (287). Walker stresses interconnectivity in her poem, "Let us be intimate with/ ancestral ghosts/ and music/ of the undead" (*Revolutionary* 68). In *The Temple of My Familiar* Walker's protagonists relate to each other, to creation, and to lives lived in the past. According to Keller, "we never begin from scratch, but with deep and difficult accumulations of past history" (114). Walker encourages her readers to keep alive the "voices of the ancestors" (*Living* 66). She believes that one of the manifestations of heaven on earth is "that where there is spiritual union with other people, the love one feels for them keeps the circle unbroken and the bond between us and them strong, whether they are dead or alive" (*Living* 67).

In a sense, the reader of *The Color Purple* is hearing the voices
of the ancestors through the authorial voice. Celie, the protagonist, speaks in a turn of the century black rural dialect
that "transforms illiterate speech into something that is, at
times, very beautiful, as well as effective in conveying her sense
of her world" (Walker, *Living* 63). In a real sense Celie's speech
itself is authorial, for according to Walker, she "speaks in the
voice and uses the language of my step-grandmother, Rachel."
Walker realizes that language defines one's world, it constructs
reality, and in the case of Celie, it reveals her inner core. Walker,
recognizing the intransparency of language, states: "Celie is
created out of language. Her being is affirmed by the language
in which she is revealed" (*Living* 64). The use of an authentic,
but individualized idiom by Celie does not allow readers to
distance themselves, nor does it allow the narrator or author
to do so. Further, Celie's language validates her existence, and
causes the reader to actually see and feel her world. Walker
defends the description of Celie's rape. She says that she "found
it almost impossible to let her say what had happened to her as
she perceived it, without euphemizing it a little. The author
herself found that once the lie that rape is pleasant was stripped
away, it was difficult to deal with the "positive horror" of the
many children "who have been sexually abused and who have
never been permitted their own language to tell about it" (*Living* 57). The use of the protagonist's language to graphically
describe sexual violence is an unusual occurrence in African
American women's literature. According to Joe Weixlmann,
"a history of experiencing sexuality in combination with violence (like rape, enforced pregnancies) influenced Black
women's attitudes towards sex," and before the late sixties made
them rather hesitant to deal with sexual subjects (170).

Barbara Christian states that the "most obvious" recurrent
theme in the works of Alice Walker is her "attention to the
black woman as creator" (*Black Feminist* 82). This is certainly
the case in *The Color Purple*. Michael Awkward describes Celie's
creative spirit as "muzzled," a spirit that exists in an environ-
ment where men try to "silence and control women" (137).
Celie is an intelligent, creative woman who has been denied
the formal education she desired. Besides the writing of her
letters, Celie also discovers that she has a talent for designing

pants, and her pants, in addition to her letters, become the symbols of her liberation. She calls her creations "Folkpants" and turns her talent into a successful business venture. In Walker's short story, "Really, Doesn't Crime Pay?," her protagonist is a female writer who gives her stories to a young man who then proceeds to steal her ideas and publish them in his own name. This woman is married to a man who does not understand her artistic talent and tries to buy her with a house and other material possessions. The woman is frustrated with her life and her husband, but decides not to kill herself. She does, however, try to kill her husband; nfortunately, the chain saw wakes him up. In desperation, after her stay in the hospital, she decides that when she is ready, she will leave his house (*In Love* 10-23). Walker's short story is written with grim humor, but in her essay "In Search of Our Mothers' Gardens," she is very serious. She speaks for the African American grandmothers and mothers who had no opportunity to express their creativity. "They were Creators, who lived lives of spiritual waste, because they were so rich in spirituality—which is the basis of Art—that the strain of enduring their unused and unwanted talent drove them insane" (*Search* 233). Walker also celebrates those women who expressed their creativity in the making of quilts, or those who, like her mother, "adorned with flowers whatever shabby house we were forced to live in" (*Search* 241). These women obviously had a need to express their creativity and had little opportunity for doing so. Thus, the everyday, often taken-for-granted household items like quilts and flowers became outlets for their artistic drive, and it is this artistic drive and creativity that they have passed to their daughters and granddaughters. Walker compares the structure of her writing to that of a crazy quilt: "A crazy-quilt story is one that can jump back and forth in time, work on many different levels, and one that can include myth" (Walker, Interview 176). Even items of clothing became a mode for expressing the artistic as well as the symbolic. Deborah McDowell states: "The use of 'clothing as iconography' is central to writings by Black women" ("New Directions" 194). Alice Walker is no exception. In *The Color Purple* Mister's sister, Kate, takes Celie to buy fabric to make a dress. Celie wants purple fabric, but there is no purple. Her second choice is red, but Kate says, "Naw, he won't want to pay for red. Too happy lookin." Celie is thrilled at the prospect of a dress. "I can't remember being the first one in my own dress" (22). When Mister rescues a very ill Shug and brings her to stay at his house, one of the first things Celie notices is her clothing. "She got on a red wool dress and chestful of black beads. A shiny black hat with what look like chickinhawk feathers curve down side one cheek, and she carrying a little snakeskin bag, match her shoes. She look like she ain't long for this world but dressed well for the next" (47). Clothing is important for expressing not only the psychological state of these women, but in *The Color Purple*, the creation of clothing becomes an artistic as well as liberating expression for Celie. Celie is rejecting her past as well as the traditional role of woman that she was forced to play.

In Walker's novel, *Meridian*, her protagonist Meridian's clothing is also symbolic. "Meridian's railroad cap and dungarees . . . are emblems of her rejection of conventional notions of womanhood" (Bröck 177). The notion of clothing as iconography may well have been passed to Walker by her "foremother" Zora Neale Hurston, for Janie Crawford's clothing is a symbol of her liberation as well. Just as Meridian's cap and dungarees are symbols of her liberation, Janie removes her "head-rag" and lets her hair flow freely down her back after Joe Starks's death (*Their Eyes* 83). The removal of the "head-rag" symbolizes Janie's freedom in much the same way that Meridian's clothing is a symbol of her freedom from patriarchal oppression. When Janie returns to Eatonville as a single independent woman, she is wearing "overhalls," a rejection of the "silken ruffles" that Starks required her to wear (*Their Eyes* 39).

While clothing is used ultimately to symbolize freedom for the female protagonists in both Hurston's and Walker's novels, Harriet Jacobs uses it as a symbol of oppression in her slave narrative. She recounts an incident that occurred after her daughter was baptized. Her father's old mistress "clasped a gold chain around my baby's neck." Jacobs recognizes that the woman wished her well, but says, "I did not like the emblem," for she saw it as a symbol of her enslaved condition (79). In another even more ironic instance, Dr. Flint proposes to give Jacobs's Brent her freedom by setting her up with a cottage of her own and providing her with light labor, "such as sewing for my family" (*Incidents* 83). Although Jacobs does not use clothing to symbolize her freedom from oppression, clothing is used as iconography in the narratives of Jacobs, Hurston, and Walker.

A final theme that recurs in Walker's novels, as well as the novels of other African American women writers, is the theme of (the) journey. "One of the central images in Black literature is the Black man on the move—on trains, in cars, on the road" (Bröck 169). While women have been traditionally portrayed as remaining at home, African American women present the motif of journey for their speaking subjects, whether the journey is inward or external. Harriet Jacobs, in *Incidents in the Life of a Slave Girl*, journeys from the plantation back to Edenton, from North Carolina to New York City and Boston, and from Boston to England and back. Janie Crawford, in Hurston's *Their Eyes Were Watching God*, journeys from her West Florida home to Eatonville, from Eatonville to the Florida Everglades, the Muck, and back to Eatonville. Hurston revises Jacobs's narrative by relating Janie's journeys to her psychological development, her sense of self. Walker signifies upon the journeys in both of these earlier texts in her novel, *The Color Purple*. Celie's journey is totally psychological. Celie "journeys" from a seemingly silent object to speaking subject. Meridian's journey is both external, as she travels about the South, and internal, as she tries to answer the question, "Could she kill?" Suwelo and Fanny both engage in journeys in *The Temple of My Familiar*. The motif of the journey may well derive from the slave narratives, but African American women writers in the twentieth century have transformed their protagonist's lives through such journeys. Just as Walker has traveled throughout the world and delved into her past for the women and men she has written about, the journeys of her creations are symbolic of the self knowledge acquired by all of Walker's women. The journeys are expressions of the search for the African American woman's spirit; a spirit that has not been destroyed by racism and sexism.

Geoffrey Wagner describes the letters written by Cecile in *Les Liaisons dangereuses* as "dramatic soliloquies, intimate revelations of herself, which she can only really recognize when they are written out." These letters are a kind of "emotional diary, or couch confession to oneself" (73). Celie's letters in *The Color Purple* serve much the same function, for in the only statement in the novel that is not incorporated into a letter, Celie's stepfather tells her, "You better not never tell nobody but God. It'd kill your mammy" (*Color* 1). Thus begin Celie's letters addressed "Dear God," and asking in the first letter for help in "letting me know what is happening to me" (*Color* 1). These are letters that function in the double discourse of reviving an epistolary style that Laclos originally used to give voice to women, and in appropriating and revising that style to give voice to a semi-literate African American woman who lived in the rural South at the turn of the century. Celie writes herself into existence through her letters while she simultaneously offers an explication of the culture in which she lives. She records the intersection of racism and sexism within the patriarchal system. More important, she also records the discourse of a community of women within the larger community. According to Lauren Berlant, Celie's narrative resists patriarchal, political language in favor of "a mode of aesthetic" representation. "These discursive modes are not 'naturally' separate, but *The Color Purple* deliberately fashions such a separation in its attempt to represent a national culture that operates according to 'womanist' values rather than patriarchal forms" (833). Celie's discourse offers the portrait of a person and a community made whole, as well as the possibilities of community and wholeness, "the spirit of everyday life relations," that women who support each other can affect (Berlant 833).

There are two semi-public narrators of *The Color Purple*. Celie is the primary narrator who finds her sister's letters and presents them to the reader approximately half-way through her epistolary narrative. Like the narrator of *Incidents in the Life of a Slave Girl*, Celie is an autodiegetic narrator. As an autodiegetic narrator she is the focus or "star" of the narrative, not merely a bystander or "walk-on" character (Genette 245). Celie cannot be considered a completely public narrator because, with the exception of the first line of the narrative in which her stepfather tells her not to tell anyone but God, the remainder of her story is in the form of letters written either to God or her sister, Nettie. While Nettie's story diverges from Celie's, Celie's is the first voice the reader encounters and her journey toward self-knowledge is the primary focus of the text. Michael Awkward refers to the "dual narrative voices of *The Color Purple*" which "become unified in much the same manner that the scraps of well-worn cloth are combined into a magnificent quilt" (161). Celie incorporates two letters into her narrative; one from her sister which she includes in a letter to God, and one from Shug which she presents in a letter to her sister, Nettie.

In addition to the two public narrators, there are two private narrators in *The Color Purple*. Just as Janie, as a private narrator, is given a brief opportunity to tell her story to Pheoby in *Their Eyes Were Watching God*, Celie allows both Squeak and Sofia to tell their experiences and observations in two of her letters to God. While these letters are private discourse and are not presented to the public by an external editor, they assume the form of a journal or diary that presents Celie's consciousness in a manner which can be read by the public. It is also worth noting that Celie maintains textual control of the letters throughout her narrative.

Janet Gurkin Altman states: "the paradox of epistolarity is that the very consistency of epistolary meaning is the interplay within a specific set of polar inconsistencies" (190). For instance, the letter format has the "power to suggest both presence and absence, to decrease and increase distance" (Altman 15).[6] Celie obviously needs to distance herself from the rape and childbirth experiences that occasion her letters. Her first fifty-one letters are addressed to God. The letters are ordered chronologically for the most part, and they are unsigned. They are undated and since they obviously were not meant to be read by anyone but Celie, they read more like journal entries than letters. *The Color Purple*, however, is not a diary novel. The diary novel does not contain the desire for exchange; however, the reader is aware from her very first letters that Celie *does* desire exchange. Celie addresses her letters to very specific narratees. The very structure of the epistolary novel relies on what Altman calls a "notion of reciprocity" or exchange between the writer and addressee (121). According to Michael Awkward, "If Altman's assertions are correct, then the epistolary narrative form, because of its intrinsic insistence upon active exchange between writer and reader, is a potentially ideal medium through which Afro-American writers can render the quintessential black verbal behavior of call-and-response"

(145).[7] This is the supreme irony of *The Color Purple*; it is written in a form that expects a response, yet there is no possibility of response nor do the protagonists expect one. The responses are contained within the textual interchange, and focus on the discursive interchange of the women of the novel. The discourse between Celie and Shug is recorded in Celie's letters and demonstrates not only Celie's development of self, but the affection that is growing between the two women. These discursive responses are eventually extended to the entire community of women within *The Color Purple* as they learn to encourage and support each other's development.

Celie's letters range in length from two short paragraphs near the beginning of the novel, to several pages as Celie's life and voice begin to unfold.[8] The reader of her letters is immediately struck by Celie's powerlessness. She has no oral voice; she exists only in her letters which simultaneously suggest both the presence and absence of her voice. The first letters serve to emphasize the isolation of Celie, a young girl who is a victim of incest, victimized by her stepfather and the patriarchal system.[9] These letters, unlike Celie's later letters, do not contain an "acute sense of audience" (Awkward 149). The letters do, however, serve a cathartic function for Celie; they enable her to distance herself from her trauma, and they also enable her to approach her trauma and herself in order that she may understand what has happened and who she is. The letters also serve to draw the reader into the narrative. According to Gates, the epistolary "form allows for a maximum of identification with a character, precisely because the devices of empathy and distance, standard in third-person narration, no longer obtain" (246). The reader is certainly aware of the intersubjective communication brought about by the epistolary form in *The Color Purple*. The careful reader is also aware of a community of discourse, a subversive addition to the usual intersubjectivity, for the women in this novel are speaking subjects who constitute their own separate discourse that is found in the humor, the pathos, and the support that they give one another.

Epistolary discourse is broken into discrete units, in which "writer and reader share neither time nor space" (Altman 135). This lack of shared time and space allows the writer to "measure and correct his words, to polish his style" (Altman 135).

In addition, since the letter is a tangible document, there are nonverbal signs that send messages about the writer and her message. The reader of *The Color Purple* is made aware of such a message in the second sentence of Celie's first letter to God. Celie tells God that she is fourteen years old. She begins her second sentence with the words "I am" but draws a line through the words and substitutes "I have always been a good girl" (*Color* 1). The reader is immediately aware of a change in her self-perception because of the line drawn through these words. The reader is also made aware of the self-reflexive nature of the document and the process of editing. For instance, Celie never calls her husband by his first name. She is not even aware of his name until she hears Shug call him Albert. Because of the nature of the epistolary form, this name appears as "Mister _____," and serves to make the reader aware not only of the distance that exists between Celie and her husband, but also of the position of servitude in which Celie is placed.

Not only does *The Color Purple* make use of the epistolary form to communicate with the reader, but Celie approaches the addressee as well as the reader through her use of language and speech patterns. She presents, in a rather informal manner, the conversations and conversational patterns of the other characters in the novel. According to Sara Mills, "the novel is less like a series of letters, but rather like a series of conversations" (70). In addition to African American dialect, the speech patterns of the characters, their voices, are presented throughout the novel. These voices, translated by Celie, are presented in direct discourse that is punctuated only with "I say," or "he or she say." The informal, conversational tone of Celie's letters makes for intimacy between writer, addressee and reader. In addition, Celie "uses certain words such as 'titties,' 'thing,' 'pussy,' which would normally only be used in intimate settings or in jokes" (Mills 71). The effect of this word usage is not only to provide an intimate glimpse of Celie's mind, but to assure that the reader will travel with Celie. In fact, the reader of *The Color Purple*, more than most epistolary novels, has a voyeuristic sense of reading messages and hearing voices that were not meant for public consumption.

Altman suggests that "even spelling can be part of the message" (135). This is certainly the case in *The Color Purple*, for Celie writes as she speaks, in dialect. For example, Celie spells kind as 'kine,' and ask as 'ast.' "As written dialogue, epistolary discourse is obsessed with its oral model" (Altman 135). Most of Celie's letters are written in present tense. One reason for this, according to Walker, is a conscious effort to preserve the "'elders' language (and it is truly astonishing how much of their language is present tense, which seems almost a message to us to remember that the lives they lived are always current, not simply historical), for it can be a light held close to them and their times, that illuminates them clearly" (*Living* 60). While Harriet Jacobs's appeal to the women of the North in *Incidents* is expressed in carefully worded standard English, Celie's letters are given power by the use of dialect.

There are two other reasons for the use of the present tense in this novel. The epistolary form itself requires the spontaneity of oral expression. For example, in her third letter to God, Celie writes of her stepfather: "He act like he can't stand me no more. Say I'm evil an always up to no good" (*Color* 4). This use of the present tense brings an immediacy to the text; the reader senses an attempt to bring past and present, absence and presence together. It is, of course, impossible to unite these opposites, for epistolary language itself is "the language of absence," and only unites through the imagination (Altman 140). The use of the present tense in unstructured letter chapters also provides a connection to the reader. According to Sara Mills, "The events are not narrated in the conventional way of situating the narrator at a particular point in time describing the events in chronological order: here the narrator is situated at the same point in time as the events—they are described as they happened with the lack of hindsight and foreshadowing which letters or a diary would have" (70). Since Celie seemingly has the same knowledge as the reader, readers have both a sense of immediacy as they read as well as empathy for the narrator.

Despite the sense of immediacy brought about by the use of the present tense in this novel, epistolary discourse is marked by a time lag between action and narration; the narrator is recording events in the past which are to be read later by the addressee. This discourse is also marked by gaps and blank spaces between letters. "Yet it is also a language of gap closing, of writing to the moment, of speaking to the addressee as if he were present" (Altman 140). Celie's first eight letters cover a period of approximately six years. She states that she is fourteen in the first letter, and her Pa puts her age at "near twenty" in the seventh letter (*Color* 9). After stating her age, however, "Pa" immediately tells "Mister _____" that, "She tell lies," so it is difficult to ascertain her age or passage of time even in this letter (*Color* 9). Celie has been silenced by the prohibition of the father, the prohibition that prefaces her letters. According to Belenky and others, silent women have "little inkling of their intellectual powers" (157). They are women who "see blind obedience to authorities as being of utmost importance for keeping out of trouble and insuring their own survival" (28). Celie is aware that she must obey in order to survive.

Even in her first letters, however, Celie indicates that she may develop the capacity to move beyond her silence. Christine Froula calls attention to the passage in which Nettie has been trying to explain the shape of the globe. "She try to tell me something bout the ground not being flat. I just say, Yeah, like I know it. I never tell her how flat it look to me" (11). This passage shows the reader the pathos of Celie's situation. It also indicates what will eventually be the source of Celie's strength, her ability to retain a sense of herself and her world. According to Froula, "Celie's eventual emergence from silence, ignorance, and misery depends upon her fidelity to the way things look to her" (Froula 638). Since the letters are undated, the reader cannot ascertain exactly how much time has passed between letters, but the very fact that they are undated is a form of authorial intrusion. The use of the present tense and lack of dating in Celie's letters is an indication of the rural South as it still exists for African Americans. These first letters also lengthen from two paragraphs to three pages. The very length of the letters indicates the growth of Celie's intellectual as well as emotional abilities.

Celie's consciousness grows as she interacts with other women in her life. On such an occasion, Celie breaks into laughter, but her laughter is silenced when "Mister _____" growls, "What you setting here laughing like a fool fer?" (*Color* 16). Celie's status is returned to that of an object by this remark. According to Lauren Berlant, however, "her split face" refers "to an object posed, but not yet constituted, the split face that produces plurivocal discourse, not a muted utterance from a victimized shadow" (846). The shared humor of the women and the subsequent anger that Celie feels toward "Mr. _____" foreshadow the voice that is to emerge. The wordplay and humor between these women, a kind of signifyin(g), binds them in community against sexism, much as it brings the larger African American community together against racism.

While Celie is unable to fight "Mr. _____" verbally, the subversive, ironic humor and parody that she shares with Nettie are early indications of Celie's growing consciousness and voice. Celie and Nettie are acting in a "womanist" manner because their humor is audacious and outrageous, and somewhat self-assured. Their behavior is reminiscent of Zora Neale Hurston's description of herself as a young girl. Hurston would sit on the gate-post to her yard and ask for rides from white travelers. She would often ride a short distance and then walk back home, always without the knowledge or permission of her parents. She states:

> "When they found out about it later, I usually got a whipping. My grandmother worried about my forward ways a great deal. She had known slavery and to her my brazenness was unthinkable" (*Dust Tracks* 34).

Hurston undoubtedly prefigured the "womanist" behavior of Walker's protagonists.

Celie's growing sense of self enables her to take her first action against the oppression of patriarchy. She is told to get Old "Mr. _____" a glass of water. She obeys but then spits in his water. Celie has become a "silent revolutionary," a woman who does not yet have the power to verbally express herself, but whose knowledge of herself is growing. Celie rebels on behalf of Shug, the woman who is to become her mother, her friend, and her lover. Nettie's letters prove to be an important aspect of *The Color Purple*. Awkward argues that one of the central themes of the novel concerns "male efforts to dominate and silence women," and that "Nettie's letters prove both in their content and in their manipulation essential factors in the author's delineation" (155). Shug and Celie recover the letters that "Mr. _____" has hidden and put them in order by their postmarks. Letters fifty-two through fifty-eight are let-

ters from Nettie to Celie. Like Celie's letters, they are undated;
unlike Celie's letters, they are signed. Both women are writing
their letters to potentially unresponsive addressees, but neither of their (written) voices can be silenced by patriarchy.
The letters which Celie reads serve another function. John F.
Callahan, in reference to African American call-and-response
patterns, argues: "To know and use your voice you need to
hear and read and interpret other voices, other stories" (20).
The letters Celie receives from Nettie, then, are as important
to her acquisition of self and voice as the discourse she shares
with Shug and Sofia.

Nettie's letters are an embedded discourse within *The Color
Purple*. Celie arranges the letters and includes them in her
narrative but presumably does not edit or revise them. Nettie,
then, becomes the second semi-public narrator of *The Color
Purple*.[10] The fifty-fifth letter in Celie's collection is the third
letter in her arrangement of letters from Nettie. This is the
first letter written from Africa. This letter is something of an
anomaly, for although the letters are all undated, this letter
does not fit into the rather rough time frame of the others.
Nettie describes seeing Sofia after she was released from prison;
however, this would have made Nettie middle-aged, and Adam
and Olivia near adulthood. Sofia did not marry Harpo until
five years after Celie married "Mr. _____." Sofia and Harpo
had five children before she left him, and has a total of six
when she reappears at Harpo's jukejoint. After she hits the
mayor of the town, she spends three years in jail before Squeak
is able to trick the sheriff into releasing Sofia into the custody
of the mayor's wife. At least fifteen years have elapsed. If Nettie
had seen Sofia in the capacity of the mayor's wife's maid, Celie's
children would have been nearly twenty years old. Also, it is
hard to imagine that Celie and Nettie would not have contacted
each other had Nettie remained in their hometown for fifteen
to twenty years. Nettie tells Celie how she is being educated by
Samuel and Corrine and how much she is reading and learning every day. She also sends words that are meant to encourage her sister: "Oh, Celie, there are colored people in the world
who want us to know! Want us to grow and see the light!" (*Color*
138). Nettie's letters not only enlarge the scope of Celie's world,
they also reflect the authorial voice. The reader is aware that

Nettie's impressions of Africa are drawn from the author's aforementioned visit.

The image of women bonding through work is one that is repeated throughout the novel. Sofia and Celie make a quilt together after Sofia confronts Celie for telling Harpo to beat her. This bonding becomes cross-sexual after "Mr. _____," initially devastated by Celie's departure, learns how to communicate intersubjectively. Near the end of the narrative, Celie and Albert actually make pants together as a symbol of their friendship. By this time "Mr. _____" has become Albert and has abandoned the role of the patriarch whose "law was unspoken, his ways immutable, and his words so close to the patriarchal script that he didn't have to finish his sentences" (Froula 641).

Keller describes Shug's statement of interconnectedness as "a clear case of oceanic feeling," that prevents her from giving up "on religion as attunement to the interconnected whole of things" (222). The narrative voice in Celie's last letters is also connected to the authorial voice. In her essay "Everything Is a Human Being," Alice Walker states: "we must begin to develop the consciousness that everything has equal rights because existence itself is equal" (*Living* 148). The spiritual essence of both narrative and authorial voices are interconnected in the narrative itself. The last letter that Celie writes is addressed to "Dear God. Dear stars, dear trees, dear sky, dear peoples. Dear Everything. Dear God" (*Color* 292). Celie writes a letter of celebration and thanksgiving for the return of her sister and children. This letter represents the (re)creation of Celie's world, and brings the narrative to the present, as much as an epistolary form can.

In her chapter on the epistolary essay, Anne Herrmann asks:

> What happens when women resort to the epistolary not for an amorous but for a dissident discourse; when they no longer seek to retrieve a male lover unchanged but seek to change the exclusionary practices of a male-dominated culture; when the letter no longer finds its inscription in a repetitive structure of desire but in a unique opportunity to advocate social change? (40).

The answer to Herrmann's question can be found in *The Color Purple*. Celie's first letters are written to a God that is patriarchal and Eurocentric by definition. As her self-knowledge and confidence develops she addresses her letters to her sister. The letter that signifies her wholeness, interconnectivity, and peace is the final one which is addressed to "Everything." The protagonists of this narrative bridge the chasm that is produced by an androcentric culture by finding within themselves the interconnectedness that enables them not only to relate to one another but to the whole of creation. Gates considers Walker's use of the epistolary form "the most stunning instance of revision in the tradition of the black novel" (xxvi). Walker's use of the epistolary form is indeed a stunning revision within the African American literary canon. In addition to its contribution to African American literature, however, *The Color Purple* is a brilliant revision, or (re)voicing of the epistolary form itself. The reader can see and hear the merging of separate texts and separate voices, in the letters of two sisters and in the narrative and authorial voices, into an interconnected and unified whole.

Chapter Four

Three Authorial Voices

The voices of the three authors under consideration, that is, Jacobs, Hurston, and Walker, in many instances speak from common experiences and perceptions that can be identified. According to bell hooks,

> "As a group, black women are in an unusual position in this society, for not only are we collectively at the bottom of the occupational ladder, but our overall social status is lower than that of any other group. Occupying such a position, we bear the brunt of sexist, racist, and classist oppression" (*Feminist* 14).

These women speak to a history that is particularly shared by African American women; however, the issues they confront and the solutions they propose concern the entire human race. They are all concerned with the problems of identity, self-definition and knowledge that face the African American woman, and it is to these problems that they address their narratives. The three authors of these narratives create, in varying degrees, woman-centered universes, universes that share certain commonalities. Their authorial and narrative voices present mind, body, and emotion in a relationship that can only be called intersubjective. By locating the commonalities, the themes as well as perspectives of the three narratives under consideration, one may be able not only to understand the interweaving of the narrative and authorial voices of these texts, but also to identify their intertextuality.

Anne Herrmann identifies the "female dialogic" in terms of "rhetorical strategies which fall outside standard genres, with a rewriting of gender which does not presuppose the heterosexual romance plot" (21). Herrmann describes a dialogic between author and character that takes the "form of a specular image—the character as both self and other—but the character functions as mask, allowing for a critique of subjectivity, leading to innovations in discursive structures" (30). The split identification, the simultaneous writing of the author/subject, the interplay between authors/protagonists, can be located in each narrative. For instance, the simultaneous voice of author and protagonists is most obvious in the closing words of *The Color Purple*. Walker, as author and medium, thanks "everybody in this book for coming." Her voice is at one with and yet distinct from those (voices) of her protagonists. This split identification gives rise to new notions of the subject and intersubjectivity in these narratives. By identifying common themes and issues that are expressed in the authorial and narratives voices of these texts, the reader can also locate the female dialogic.

One theme easily identified in all three narratives is that of the desire of the protagonists for "ethical self-governance".[1] Bonnie St. Andrews describes ethical self-governance: "For those engaged in the study of Literature, the desire for 'knowledge of good and evil' is a fundamental issue" (vii). Only those individuals who possess a 'knowledge of good and evil' are at liberty to make ethical and moral decisions. "In myths and stories—sacred and secular tales—women and knowledge seem the fateful conjunction" (St. Andrews 1). The narratives of Jacobs, Hurston and Walker present female protagonists who engage in a quest for self-knowledge and ultimately speak from a position of self-governance. Each of these women challenge, and break, existing laws or mores in the process of developing an independent conscience, for in the process of seeking self-governance, each recognizes another, equally ethical necessity. Harriet Jacobs leaves her master in pursuit of freedom, Janie Killicks leaves her husband in pursuit of self-knowledge, and Celie not only leaves her husband, but has a relationship with another woman, in an effort to achieve self-knowledge and self-governance. These women also challenge and modify existing myths concerning women and ethical knowledge.

In *Incidents in the Life of a Slave Girl*, Harriet Jacobs challenges her master's power over her body. She tells this man that he has "'no right to do as you like with me'" (*Incidents* 39). She resolves never to give in to the demands of her master; instead, she decides to take another lover of her own choosing. "I knew what I did, and I did it with deliberate calculation" (54). Just as Jacobs moves beyond the sexual demands of her master by denying him access to her body, she physically moves from his grasp by successfully escaping to the North. In the years before Emancipation, Jacobs was located by her master's daughter. From a position of ethical self-governance, she states: "I knew the law would decide that I was his property . . . but I regarded such laws as the regulations of robbers, who had no rights that I was bound to respect" (187). In both instances, she flouts the accepted moral and adjudicated law. Eudora Welty used the term "ironic modification" to indicate "how myths and secular stories serve the purposes of a particular writer" (St. Andrews 12).[2] Jacobs uses the myth of the "cult of true womanhood" and addresses the "true woman's" attributes of purity, piety, submissiveness, and domesticity at the same instance that she "confesses" herself either unable or unwilling to fulfill those very attributes. The use of this mythic structure enables her to communicate her plight to her readers. Although Jacobs gives lip-service to the cult of true womanhood, the underlying message to her reader is that of ethical self-governance. Not only does she challenge her master, but through him the whole system of patriarchy that chattelized both women and Africans. While the younger Jacobs insisted on self-governance by escaping to the North, the reader can hear the voice of self-governance in the narrative of the older Jacobs, the author of *Incidents in the Life of a Slave Girl*. The voice of ethical self-governance from the author and protagonist of *Incidents* is an example of the female dialogic.

Jacobs directs her challenge to an external, white audience, but Zora Neale Hurston's voice is directed to the African American community itself. In *Their Eyes Were Watching God*, Hurston, through her protagonist Janie Crawford Killicks Stark Woods, directly challenges not only the accepted mores and conventions of the African American community of Eatonville but those of her readers in general. Janie, who is pressured into marrying Logan Killicks, gives little thought to walking away from her first husband to marry her second. She is persuaded to marry Joe Starks because of what St. Andrews terms "the myth of sustaining love" (13). Joe Starks did not represent the ideal love that Janie saw in the blossoming pear tree, but he "spoke for far horizon" (*Their Eyes* 28). Starks also represented material well-being, and traditional male/female roles within a "happily ever after" scenario. Hurston engages in an ironic modification of this scenario, for Janie, in a manner similar to that of Kate Chopin's heroine, "awakens."[3] Janie also leaves respectability and responsibility when she marries Tea Cake and settles for a life of migrant work on the Muck of the Florida Everglades. Janie declares her ethical independence when she tells Pheoby, "Two things everybody's got tuh do fuh theyselves. They got tuh go tuh God, and they got tuh find out about livin' fuh theyselves" (*Their Eyes* 183). This is an example of female dialogic, for Hurston's authorial voice speaks through Janie's declaration of self-governance. Hurston herself claimed to have "touched the four corners of the horizon" (*Dust Tracks* 255). Hurston cared little about fulfilling traditional female roles. Indeed, she actively fought against subordination and silence. In *Their Eyes Were Watching God*, the voice is self-reflexive, for it is spoken by the author as well as the protagonist, and it urges the African American woman, indeed all women, to move beyond their traditional roles of silence and subordination.

Celie, the protagonist of Alice Walker's *The Color Purple*, actually "awakens" herself. In other words, she writes herself "into creation," into consciousness. The reader is able to trace the evolution of her ethical self-governance through her letters. Unlike Janie, Celie is unaware of the "myth of sustaining love" (St. Andrews 13). She is neither courted nor consulted in the matter of her mate, but is traded like property to "Mr. _____." Shug enables Celie to develop ethical self-governance by teaching her to love and value herself. Celie declares her ethical independence in her final letter which she addresses: "Dear God. Dear stars, dear trees, dear sky, dear peoples. Dear Everything. Dear God" (*Color* 292). Because Celie eventually surrounds herself with a community of women, she seemingly does not face the possible criticism and condemnation that threatens Linda Brent and Janie Woods. The reader of *The Color Purple*, however, is aware that Celie, like Linda and Janie, abandons her traditional role and respectability when she renounces "Mr. _____" and heterosexual love for a relationship with Shug. Actually, Celie has more moral freedom than either Linda Brent or Janie Woods.

Like Hurston, Walker speaks against the subordination and silencing of women, and like Hurston, Walker believes that "We are *indeed* the world" (*Living* 193). The female dialogic is evident in *The Color Purple* as Walker's authorial voice speaks through Celie's last letter, the letter in which she declares her own ethical self-governance. Walker reaffirms her personal self-governance in her essay, "The Universe Responds." She states that the physical world is inseparable "from the divine; and everything, *especially* the physical world, is divine" (*Living* 192).

Because *The Color Purple* was written after the Civil Rights Movement of the 1960's and the Women's Liberation Movement of the 1970's, Walker is able to construct a somewhat separate community of women, a community based on mutual respect and love. Walker has more freedom to express her creativity than either Jacobs or Hurston. She has not been bound by a mythical code of "true womanhood" as Jacobs was in the nineteenth century, nor have her novels been undervalued and criticized by both Anglo and African American literary critics as were Hurston's in the 1930's.[1] When Walker's protagonist, Celie, develops enough self-knowledge to understand and validate her emotions, she never questions or offers explanation for her moral self-governance. While all three authors advocate moral self-governance, only Walker, writing in the last quarter of the twentieth century, is able to propose complete moral self-governance for herself as well as her protagonist. Although nineteenth century cultural mores allowed women to form deep and loving friendships that often lasted a lifetime, of the three authors under consideration only Walker has had the freedom to propose a sexual lesbian relationship based on love and mutual understanding for her protagonists. Moral self-governance by the "daughters of Eve," based on the knowledge of good and evil, is a major challenge for those who are intent on abolishing or revising the patriarchal system.

A common theme that can be located in each of the three narratives under consideration is that of resistance to domination. An examination of the protest by the protagonists of these three narratives reveals the authorial voices as well as cultural expressions of that protest. Although Harriet Jacobs records that she protested verbally to Dr. Flint's attempt to sexually dominate her, she also protested in other ways. When Dr. Flint upbraided her after the birth of her second baby, heaping upon her "every vile epithet he could think of", she "fainted at his feet" (*Incidents* 77). It is possible that Jacobs fainted from weakness, but the image is one of mute protest. The doctor threw cold water on her and shook her to restore her to consciousness. Jacobs continues that she "suffered in consequence of this treatment; but I begged my friends to let me die. There was nothing I dreaded so much as his presence" (*Incidents* 78). The image Jacobs presents is that of the hysterical woman of the nineteenth century. According to Carroll Smith-Rosenberg, nineteenth century women "'chose' the character traits of hysteria as their particular mode of expressing malaise, discontent, anger, or pain" (198). They reacted in these ways, often by taking to their beds with seizures, depression, and/or weakness for days or even years, because they felt powerless to resist male domination in any other manner. Jacobs was, in an indirect and, by modern standards, somewhat pathological manner, asserting her own power by stating that she would "rather die" than be dominated. Jacobs was addressing a body of women who were undoubtedly familiar with her form of illness/protest.[5]

While Jacobs uses images of hysteria to protest the domination of Dr. Flint, Hurston uses absence or withdrawal. She also uses images of the body to signal Janie's liberation from male domination. In *Their Eyes Were Watching God*, Nanny, Janie's grandmother, silences her granddaughter's protest against marrying Logan Killicks with violence. When Killicks later threatens her with violence, Janie simply walks away from the farm to join Joe Starks and start a new life in Florida. Janie does not physically leave Starks when he silences her, but she withdraws from him. "No matter what Jody did, she said nothing. She had learned how to talk some and leave some" (*Their Eyes* 72). Janie "got nothing from Jody except what money could buy, and she was giving away what she didn't value" (*Their Eyes* 72). Janie protests Joe's domination over her by burning "up every one of her head rags" after his death (*Their Eyes* 85).

Janie resists the community's efforts to force her into a respectable marriage after Joe's death and finally leaves for the Muck, the Florida Everglades, with a seeming ne'er-do-well, Tea Cake. She uses her body to symbolize her final liberation. She allows her hair to fall freely down her back, and she disposes of the dresses Joe bought her in favor of the faded shirt and muddy overalls that so shocks the town of Eatonville upon her return. Janie's form of protest resembles Jacobs's in that it is private and individualized; neither of these two women give active voice to their protests in the manner of Alice Walker's protagonists.

Celie, Walker's protagonist of *The Color Purple*, protests the abuse she suffers by writing letters to God. Although the letters are private and not meant to be read, Celie asks for active intervention. This request for action immediately distinguishes Celie's protest from the more passive protests of Harriet Jacobs and Janie Woods. In her early letters, Celie remains outwardly silent and protests in subversive ways. As the women of *The Color Purple* begin to dialogue with each other, their protests become not only more verbal but also more active and effective. Their protests are in response to manifestations of both racism and sexism. Sofia protests the way Harpo treats her with the words, "He don't want a wife, he want a dog" (*Color* 68). She further protests her treatment at the hands of the white community when she tells Celie, "They won't let me see no mens. Well, after five years they let me see you once a year. I'm a slave. What would you call it?" (*Color* 108). Celie finally protests the physical abuse of "Mr. _____," by telling Shug, "He beat me when you not here" (*Color* 78). The mutual support of the women in this novel makes their protest effective. They not only encourage and advise one another, they take action on behalf of their sisters. When Celie tells Shug that "Mr. _____" beats her, Shug promises to stay until "I know Albert won't even think about beating you" (*Color* 79). When Mary Agnes decides to go with Shug to Memphis in order to pursue a singing career, Sofia offers to take care of her child. These women refuse to succumb to jealousy and competition. The lack of jealousy and the mutual support among this community of women, allows them to actively voice their protest. The discourse of these women enables them to become signifying subjects, and the resulting relationships that they form move them into intersubjectivity. These women not only protest verbally and actively but as speaking and/or writing subjects, they demonstrate what may be termed unconventional emotions. The protest against domination in these three narratives is an expression of both authorial and narrative voice, for Jacobs, Hurston, and Walker have verbally and actively protested in their public writing and in their private lives. The interplay of authors and protagonists as they protest domination within narratives that do not "presuppose the heterosexual romance plot" is an expression of the female dialogic (Herrmann 30).

The reader of all three narratives is aware of the anger, indeed outrage, of the authorial and narrative voices. Just as the authorial/narrative voices of the works under consideration have protested domination as an expression of the female dialogic, these voices also express anger and outrage at racism and sexism within their respective societies. Jacobs, Hurston, and Walker use their anger and outrage at racism and sexism to create self-reflexive narratives in which their protagonists find at least partial solutions to the social dilemmas they face. According to Alison M. Jaggar, "Race, class, and gender shape every aspect of our lives, and our emotional constitution is not excluded" (157). Jaggar argues that people who are oppressed because of their race, class and/or gender are often unable to experience conventional emotions. Because of their position in society they most often experience "outlaw" emotions, and these very emotions can aid in "forming a subculture defined by perceptions, norms, and values that systematically oppose the prevailing perceptions, norms, and values." The authors and narrators of all three narratives under consideration exhibit feminist emotions, "emotions that exhibit feminist perceptions and values" (Jaggar 160). They also exhibit emotions that are responses to class and race victimization.

In depicting her struggle with her master, Linda Brent, Jacobs's protagonist asks, "Reader, did you ever hate? I hope not." She compares her feelings to the "'atmosphere of hell'" and expresses the hope that she never has such feelings toward another person again (*Incidents* 40). These feelings are a response to Dr. Flint's proscription that Brent might never again see her lover, the free black that she had hoped to eventually marry. Her feelings are a result of the double bind of racism and sexism. As a slave she was not free to court or marry the man of her choice, and as a slave woman she faced constant sexual harassment from her master. It is reasonable to assume that Jacobs obscures reality somewhat by implying that Dr. Flint was unsuccessful in his attempts to rape or seduce her. According to Fox-Genovese, "it stretches the limits of all credulity that Linda Brent actually eluded her master's sexual advances" (*Plantation* 392). If she was, indeed, unable to elude these advances, Jacobs's emotions and voice would reflect outrage over her lack of freedom of choice. Although Jacobs's emotions are easily understood by a twentieth century reader, Jacobs felt the need to justify her feelings to her reader. According to Jaggar, conventionally unacceptable emotions, "may lead us to make subversive observations that challenge dominant conceptions of the status quo" (161). While Jacobs writes within boundaries that would be acceptable to white northern women, she defends both her emotions and actions with the observation: "I feel that the slave woman ought not to be judged by the same standard as others" (*Incidents* 56). After Brent arrives in the North, she encounters prejudice and racial discrimination. Her anger is obvious as she writes: "I found it hard to preserve my self-control" (*Incidents* 176). In both situations, Jacobs responds appropriately to her emotions. Her hatred for her master causes her to escape his domination, and her anger over racial discrimination causes her to resist her oppressors. Her anger is expressed first on behalf of African Americans who have suffered oppression, and then within the confines of the "cult of true womanhood" when expressed on behalf of women.

In *Their Eyes Were Watching God*, Janie Starks responds to Joe's belittling remarks about women's inability to think. Her response reflects feminist anger: "Ah knows uh few things, and womenfolks thinks sometimes too!" Janie "fought back with her tongue" but to no avail. Janie feels anger at the men's disparaging remarks and "good-natured laughter at the expense of women" (*Their Eyes* 68). Her feminist anger surfaces when she finally tells Joe to "stop mixin' up mah doings wid mah looks" (*Their Eyes* 74). While Janie's voice is confined to her fictive community, her emotions reflect the authorial voice. According to Gates, Hurston's is a "*divided* voice, a double voice unreconciled, that strikes me as her great achievement, a verbal analogue of her double experiences as a woman in a male-dominated world and as a black person in a nonblack world" (*Their Eyes* 193). Like Jacobs, Hurston's anger is most directly aimed at racism, the oppression of African Americans. In her essay, "Seeing the World as It Is," she speaks against racism. "I just think it would be a good thing for the Anglo-Saxon to get the idea out of his head that everybody else owes him something just for being blonde" (*Their Eyes* 251). Hurston never reveals her own, "personal" feminist anger, but since she speaks directly against the oppression of African Americans, her reader may correctly conclude that her voice also speaks through Janie's "feminist" anger.

In *The Color Purple*, Celie feels tremendous anger at "Mr. _____" for concealing her sister's letters for many years. She is actually recognizing concealed emotions, emotions that are contained but not acknowledged in her letters. She emerges as an outraged woman who asks, "How I'm gon keep from killing him" (150). Celie is angry at men in general and God, who she sees as a man, in particular. Shug helps Celie to deal with her anger against men and God by telling her, "you have to git man off your eyeball, before you can see anything a'tall" (204). According to Jaggar, "When certain emotions are shared or validated by others, the basis exists for forming a subculture defined by perceptions, norms, and values that systematically oppose the prevailing perceptions, norms, and values" (160). Celie is supported by a community of women who validate and encourage one another's emotions and creativity. Walker encourages a sisterhood among African American women that involves dialogue. "I believe in listening—to a person, the sea, the wind, the trees, but especially to young black women whose rocky road I am still traveling" (*Search* 272). Jaggar argues that women and other oppressed people have a less partial, more objective perspective of reality "and therefore a better chance of ascertaining the possible beginnings of a society in which all could thrive" (162). The feminist dialogue in these three works, perhaps more than any other aspect, is the most forceful expression of the female dialogic. The women in these narratives, in their discourse, encourage each other, provide role-models for each other, and work toward the establishment of a sisterhood of mutual support.[6]

The dialogue between women in the works under consideration differs from dialogue between males, and, with one exception, between males and females. The women in these narratives talk about their troubles and exchange confidences with one another. The intersubjective dialogue of these authorial/ narrative voices reject the traditional heterosexual romance plot and speak/write new spaces in which the female protagonists create interactive dialogue with one another. According to Daniel N. Maltz and Ruth A. Borker, females create friendships of closeness and equality through dialogue by allowing others to speak and acknowledging and supporting what they say. The resulting exchange of experiences and confidences produces mutual commitment within a sexually differentiated communicative culture (205). The dialogue between women in these narratives, then, is intersubjective, and based on equality and empathy between listener and speaker.

In *Incidents in the Life of a Slave Girl,* Linda Brent relates several conversations she has with Betty, the servant of the woman who hid Brent after her escape from Dr. Flint's plantation. Betty is her connection with the outside world, the woman who brings the news that Brent's children have been bought by their father and who rejoices with Linda at the news. "Brudder, chillern, all is bought by de daddy! I'se laugh more dan nuff, tinking 'bout ole massa Flint. Lor, how he *vill* swar!" (*Incidents* 108). While Betty shares Brent's sense of fear for herself and concern for her children, it is the dialogue between Brent and her daughter that reveals most clearly the intersubjective relationship that women often form. Brent decides to tell her daughter, Ellen, about her affair with Mr. Sand and the births of her two children. As Brent recounts her story, her daughter interrupts to assure her that she knows who her father is, but that "All my love is for you." Brent, who is grateful for her daughter's love and support, wishes she had spoken to her long ago, "for my pent-up feelings had often longed to pour themselves out to some one I could trust" (*Incidents* 189). The dialogue between these women is mutually supportive;

even though Ellen interrupts her mother's confession, she does so only to reassure her mother and acknowledge the hurt she has suffered. Her interruption is a response, not a method of gaining power or dominance in the conversation.[7] The conversation between Brent and her daughter, which Brent calls "The Confession," belies its title, for the conversation is interactive, with two speaking subjects engaging in reciprocal discourse, not one person confessing to an authority figure. This dialogue, like much of the dialogue in *Incidents*, exists on the margins of culture and is reciprocal in nature; thus, it is an expression of the female dialogic.

In *The Color Purple*, Celie speaks about her feelings for the first time in a dialogue with Shug. Shug and Celie discuss their feelings for "Mr. _____." Shug asks Celie how she feels about Shug and Albert sleeping together. Celie replies that Shug "might git big again" (*Color* 80). The two women discuss their feelings for Albert and their sexual relations with him. Shug explains that she has "what you call a passion" for Albert, and from Celie's reply, she realizes that Celie has never enjoyed a sexual experience. "Why Miss Celie, she say, you still a virgin" (*Color* 81). This exchange of personal feelings cements the mutual commitment of the two women. The speech strategies in this dialogue that are specific to women's language include extensive use of personal and inclusive pronouns like 'you' and 'I,' explicit responses to what has just been said, and the interjection of comments and questions during a speaker's discourse (Maltz & Borker 210). In fact, there are thirteen questions asked within this one dialogue that are designed to elicit a response from the other subject and six of them are questions about feelings. These strategies not only create continuity in the conversation, but they are similar to the engaging strategies used by Harriet Jacobs, strategies that elicit empathy from the addressee. The mutual reciprocity, the marginality, and the untraditional subject matter of the discourse of these women are a part of the female dialogic. Like Linda Brent and her daughter, these two women are exchanging not only information in an interactive manner, but they are forming a relationship of equality that will endure.

The first woman-to-woman dialogue in *Their Eyes Were Watching God* takes place on the steps of Janie Woods' back porch.

Janie's friend, Pheoby Watson, brings her a plate of "mulatto rice" and a welcome home from her journey. Janie, full of "self-revelation" proceeds to tell Pheoby the story of her life. While the dialogue is a function of the framing device of the narration, it contains characteristics similar to those found in the other two narratives. The conversation is interactive, focuses on the feelings of the two women, and reveals the mutual trust and commitment that is felt between the women. Indeed, Janie gives Pheoby permission to tell her story to the townspeople. "You can tell 'em what Ah say if you wants to. Dat's just de same as me 'cause mah tongue is in mah friend's mouf." The trust and empathy between these two "kissin'-friends" has allowed their friendship to endure for twenty years (*Their Eyes* 6). Janie gives Pheoby permission to speak for her in a gesture of ultimate reciprocity, an expression of the female dialogic.

Not all the conversations between women in this narrative are between friends. Janie also has a conversation with Mis' Turner, a light-skinned woman who hates blacks and who cannot understand why Janie is married to a dark-skinned man. The two women do not communicate with the same reciprocity that characterized the other conversations between women; nevertheless, their dialogue contains elements of female communicative culture. As Mis' Turner voices her racism in a fanatical manner, Janie responds politely and punctuates the conversation with questions or brief comments until Mis' Turner announces that Booker T. Washington "wuz a white folks' nigger." "According to all Janie had been taught this was sacrilege so she sat without speaking at all" (*Their Eyes* 136). Janie distances herself from Mis' Turner by using her title and by skirting the issue or remaining silent when confronted by what she considers "blasphemy" (*Their Eyes* 136). Obviously, Janie does not agree with what is being said; therefore, her voice is silent. The reader is also aware of the presence of the authorial voice in this dialogue. Hurston speaks disparagingly of those African Americans who consider themselves superior because of skin color or education. In her essay entitled "My People, My People," she ridicules the phenomenon of "passing," and announces that "you can't tell who my people are by skin color" (*Dust Tracks* 216). The dialogue between Janie and Mis' Turner demonstrates the interplay of the authorial/narrative voice that is a reflection of the female dialogic.

The three narratives under consideration not only speak to the female communicative process, they also contain information about men to women and men to men speech strategies. According to Maltz and Borker, a common characteristic of male speaking patterns is the tendency toward narratives such as jokes and stories that are performances for audiences. The male narratives or "mule stories" in Hurston's *Their Eyes Were Watching God* were always "performed," usually before a male audience. These performances were often characterized by competition between the men either for the most outrageous or the funniest narrative. Two other characteristics of male speech are "loud and aggressive arguments" and "practical jokes, challenges, put-downs, insults, and other forms of verbal aggression" (Maltz and Borker 212). Among the three narratives, the only extended dialogues that involve only men are found in *Their Eyes Were Watching God.*

Sam Watson and Lige Moss are well known for their "eternal arguments," arguments that take place on the porch in front of the store. Their arguments are loud and aggressive and are punctuated with put-downs. In an argument over whether nature or caution keeps a person from getting burned by a stove, Sam tells Lige, "Ah'm gointuh run dis conversation from uh gnat heel to uh lice. It's nature dat keeps uh man off of uh red-hot stove." Lige responds, "T'ain't no sich uh thing! Nature tells you not tuh fool wid no red-hot stove" (*Their Eyes* 60). The men continue their argument until the porch is "boiling" with phrases like "Dat's uh lie" and "Naw it ain't neither" (*Their Eyes* 61). Unlike the supportive, reciprocal speech of women, the men of Eatonville exchange challenges as well as good-natured verbal abuse. While Jacobs and Walker exclude male dialogue from their narratives, Hurston includes many instances of male speech strategies in her novel. Hurston's narrative has a somewhat different purpose from the other two; in this narrative the author obviously wishes to demonstrate the dominance of men in this culture and the damage such dominance does to women. According to Mary Helen Washington, "The language of the men in *Their Eyes* is almost always divorced from any kind of interiority, and the men are rarely shown in the process of growth" (Foreword xiii). Since the novel is woman-centered, and Janie is shown in the process

of growth, the male speech patterns reveal not only static characters, but characters whose speech is almost stereotypical.

Since men and women have different speech strategies and
cultural rules for friendly conversation, they often encounter
conflict when they converse. Deborah Tannen has concluded
that men and women speak different languages. She states: "If
women speak and hear a language of connection and intimacy,
while men speak and hear a language of status and independence, then communication between men and women can be
like cross-cultural communication, prey to a clash of conversational styles" (42). Males tend to seek status within their worlds,
and the best way to achieve and maintain status is to give orders (Tannen 47). Joe Starks demonstrates such speech strategies in *Their Eyes Were Watching God*. Joe wants Janie to tie up
her hair because he is jealous of the other men who admire it.
He orders Janie to tie up her hair. But he never explains why.
"It just wasn't in him" (52). When Janie tells Joe that their life
together in the community of Eatonville keeps them from being "natural wid one 'nother," Joe responds to her plea for
intimacy with "Ah ain't even started good." Joe has plans to
acquire status, to be "a big voice" in the community; he also
states that Janie should be happy because "dat makes uh big
woman outa you" (43). The man and woman in this dialogue
are not communicating. Joe responds to Janie's desire for intimacy by reaffirming his desire for status and independence.
The two are talking at cross purposes, stymied by what Tannen
calls "different genderlects" (42). While linguists such as
Tannen, Maltz, and Borker note the differences in speech patterns, they do not suggest that these differences are physiologi-
cal in nature. The implication is that they are learned responses
within an androcentric society.[8]

The narrators of *Their Eyes Were Watching God* and *Incidents
in the Life of a Slave Girl* record male-female conversations in
which reciprocity and empathy are totally absent. When Janie
dares to "talk back" to Joe, to address him in the same manner
he has been accustomed to address her, he totally withdraws
and loses his will to live. When Linda Brent "sasses" Dr. Flint,
he threatens her life and eventually strikes her (*Incidents* 39).
These conversations are stripped of any desire for reciprocity
and are motivated by raw power and total dominance. Walker's

narrative, however, moves beyond the androcentric hierarchical relationships that are described in Celie's first letters to a more intersubjective stance that is validated by interactive language. Walker's *The Color Purple*, like the other two narratives, is descriptive in that it presents racism and sexism in an extremely realistic manner. Walker, however, becomes prescriptive as Celie's knowledge of self and world develop. The men and women of *The Color Purple* are finally able to bridge the incommensurabilities, or communicative chasms, that separate them.

Carol Gilligan stresses that the differences between female and male voices, "arise in a social context where factors of social status and power combine with reproductive biology to shape the experience of males and females and the relations between the sexes" (2). In like manner Nancy Chodorow points to "the fact that women, universally, are largely responsible for early child care" to explain why females tend to define themselves "in relation and connection to other people more than masculine personality does" (43). Walker, unlike her predecessors, presents the reader with the differences in male and female voice, and then demonstrates the possibilities of bridging the gap between them. The reader can hope that Walker's prescription for communicative bridging between the sexes is not a fairy tale ending to an improbable future, but a model of possibilities for all men and women.

While Walker's community of women point the way toward bridging communicative chasms, they do not cease to interact with men. Celie, who finds sexual fulfillment within a lesbian relationship, discovers that she is able after many years and more maturity, to develop an interactive dialogue with Albert. Albert, on the other hand, finally recognizes the beauty in Celie, and is able to establish a connective relationship with her. The great accomplishment of *The Color Purple* is that, ultimately, there are no "bad guys" in it, just people who have learned to listen to each other's voices.

Harriet Jacobs and Zora Neale Hurston, in part because of societal limitations placed upon their voices, do not propose strategies that would open racial or gender lines of communication. Jacobs (appropriately) encourages resistance to racism and segregation in the North. Her narrative ends on a note of isolation: "The dream of my life is not yet realized. I do not sit with my children in a home of my own. I still long for a hearth-stone of my own, however humble" (*Incidents* 201). Hurston's protagonist, Janie, achieves independence and self-knowledge, but her "freedom" is in the form of personal liberation. Like Jacobs's narrative, *Their Eyes Were Watching God*, ends with an isolated heroine. Alone in her bedroom, comforted only by the memory of Tea Cake, Janie "pulled in her horizon like a great fish-net. Pulled it from around the waist of the world and draped it over her shoulder. So much of life in its meshes! She called in her soul to come and see" (*Their Eyes* 184). The gendered relationships of both authors' protagonists remained asymmetrical throughout the narratives. It is untenable, then, that they could possibly have maintained such relationships and also emerged as self-actualized heroines.

Unlike Jacobs and Hurston, Walker's protagonist, Celie, does not emerge as an isolated heroine. Her voice, her self-knowledge, and the freedom that she acquires is an integral part of the novel's community of women. According to Fox-Genovese, "to abandon 'free' as the product of collective experience is to abandon the cultural, social and political contest that gives meaning to the individual story" (*Feminism* 220). The reader actually hears a "plurality of voices," at the novel's end, a plurality that not only reflects the voices of Celie, Shug, and Nettie, but a plurality that also bridges the chasm of gender. This plurality of voices which is demonstrating reciprocity as well as speaking from a marginalized community is certainly an expression of the female dialogic.

These authors not only reveal the communicative chasms that divide men and women, they also attempt to bridge a language chasm that divides the African American community from the dominant culture. If language creates the limits of our world, if as Dale Spender contends, it is "both a creative and an inhibiting vehicle," these women write within two paradoxes. According to Spender, "Males, as the dominant group, have produced language, thought and reality" (143). Thus, as women and speaking subjects, the authors of the narratives under consideration are expressing themselves through the language of the/an Other. Second, as members of a minority group which was once enslaved in this country, they are ex-

pressing themselves through the language of another, dominant group. Elizabeth Fox-Genovese asks: "How do you write
your self in someone else's words? in another people's words?"
(*Feminism* 207). In a sense, these writers express themselves
through a triple consciousness. As African Americans and as
women, they write within two oppressive systems, using the
language of their oppressors. The are able, however, to cre-
atively use the language to communicate a different perspective to their readers.

Although Jacobs, Hurston, and Walker do not all bridge the
communicative chasm that separates the sexes, they are all
forced, to some extent, to bridge the chasm that separates their
ethnic community from that of the dominant society. According to Fox-Genovese, as African American writers they engage
in an "act of translation" that "further commits them, whatever their intentions, to viewing their people's community
through the eyes of the observer" (209). This act of translation
takes place within an African American literary tradition that
has "complex double formal antecedents, the Western and the
black" and is noted for its process of "signifyin(g)" upon previous texts, both oral and written (Gates xxiv). The attempts
to communicate across ethnic divisions are as varied among
these writers as were their attempts to communicate across
gender divisions.

Harriet Jacobs, while using dialect to describe the speech
of other slaves, does not allow her protagonist, Linda Brent, to
speak in dialect. As Fox-Genovese points out, Harriet Jacobs
"took great pains to differentiate her protagonist, Linda Brent,
from the ordinary women of the slave community, whose own
admirable qualities she depicted" (*Feminism* 211). There are
two reasons for this differentiation. Jacobs needed to establish herself as author and authority, and she also needed to
establish herself as a respectable woman. As stated earlier,
Jacobs was writing to women of the North, to ask for help for
those still in bondage. Her use of engaging strategies, of appealing directly to the reader for empathy, as well as her use
of language were a part of this appeal. For the modern reader,
her narrative strategies and language use seem somewhat awkward and stilted; however, her work is remarkable considering
the confines of the literary tradition within which she wrote.

Although Jacobs faced difficulties in publishing and marketing her narrative, today's reader cannot measure the success of her narrative strategies by the nineteenth century reception of her narrative. According to Jean Fagan Yellin, Jacobs creates a "new voice" and "projects a new kind of female hero" (*Incidents* xiv). This voice was to inspire other African American female writers to create heroic female protagonists.

Zora Neale Hurston, unlike Jacobs, has the freedom to allow her protagonist, Janie Crawford Killicks Starks Woods, to speak through the African American dialect. Hurston, writing almost eighty years after *Incidents* was published, makes use of her education and anthropological background to recreate the community in which she grew up. Her novel, then, is autobiographical and her use of third person narrative voice as well as free indirect discourse, allows her to express emotions that she dismisses in her official autobiography. Since her narrative voice can be considered a "private" one, and since Hurston lived in a society in which African American women had little, if any, power, her narrative remains descriptive. While she introduces protagonists who speak in dialect, it is worth noting that the third person narrative voice uses standard English. According to Gates, however, in her use of free indirect discourse, "Hurston showed the tradition just how dialect could blend with standard English to create a new voice, a voice exactly as black as it is white" (251). Thus, Hurston does build bridges that connect the discourses of two language groups. She implicitly challenges the dominant culture of white Protestant America and she explicitly challenges the patriarchal dominance that her protagonist, Janie, faced. She does not, however, offer methods for bridging the chasm that separates the sexes in her novel. Janie remains alone, an individualized, autonomous heroine, much like Hurston herself.

Of the three authors, only Alice Walker offers the possibilities of bridging both racial and gender gaps. Her protagonists speak the dialect of their heritage. The use of dialect in Celie's letters, however, has the effect of drawing the reader into her mind and emotions. According to Gates, Walker brings before us, "a writing style of such innocence with which only the most hardened would not initially sympathize, then eventually *empathize*" (246). A part of Celie's writing style is the seeming "naturalness" of her language. Walker not only demonstrates the possibilities of bridging language gaps between ethnic groups, but she also shows the reader how males and females can learn to communicate effectively with one another. The bridging of communicative chasms is one of the most powerful prescriptions offered by *The Color Purple*.

The three authors under consideration, Jacobs, Hurston, and Walker, present images of androgyny in their narratives. In *Incidents* and *Their Eyes*, however, the authorial and narrative voices do not resolve these images into a harmonious whole. For instance, Harriet Jacobs's flight from the plantation, her disguise as a sailor, and her ship-board journey to the North, may be considered "masculine" activities, while her unwillingness to leave her children, and her occupation as seamstress can be considered "feminine" (*Incidents* 95-158). Hurston's Janie also exhibits "masculine" behavior when she walks away from Logan Killicks's farm, when she accompanies Tea Cake to the Muck, and when she reappears in Eatonville wearing overalls (*Their Eyes* 31, 122, 2). Her seeming willingness to allow her third husband, Teacake, to beat her can be considered "feminine" behavior. These "masculine" and "feminine" behaviors are simply presented and left under tension in Jacobs's and Hurston's narratives. Alice Walker, on the other hand, bridges the gender chasm to present images of androgyny as images of wholeness.

According to Marie H. Buncombe, "Walker uses androgyny as a metaphor for the 'wholeness,' the totality of the black experience as she sees it" (420). In her essay, "In the Closet of the Soul," Walker describes her protagonists, Celie and Albert, from *The Color Purple*:

> The point is, neither of these people is healthy. They are, in fact, dreadfully ill, and they manifest their dis-ease according to their culturally derived sex roles and the bad experiences early impressed on their personalities. They proceed to grow, to change, to become whole, i.e., well, by becoming more like each other, but stopping short of talking on each other's illness. Celie becomes more self-interested and aggressive; Albert becomes more thoughtful and considerate of others" (*Living* 80).

In other words, Celie and Albert become more androgynous. Celie becomes more assertive. She leaves Albert to live with

Shug in Memphis, she begins to make folkpants, and eventually goes into business for herself. Albert, known earlier to Celie as "Mr. _____," changes also. He learns to cook and makes yam dishes for Henrietta, Sofia's daughter who is suffering from a "blood disease." Celie states: "Sometime I meet up with "Mr._____" visiting Henrietta. He dream up his own little sneaky recipes. For instance, one time he hid the yams in peanut butter" (*Color* 259). "Mr. _____" and Celie become friends as they become more androgynous, and eventually they make folkpants together. They do not, however, remarry because Celie remains lesbian. She states: "Take off they pants, I say, and men look like frogs to me" (*Color* 261). Walker calls for a redefinition of terms like "masculine," "feminine," and "lesbian," "since the conventional meanings have led to polarization, fear, and hostility," within the African American community (Buncombe 420). In her essay, "Breaking Chains and Encouraging Life," Walker states: "perhaps black women writers and nonwriters should say, simply, whenever black lesbians are being put down, held up, messed over, and generally told their lives should not be encouraged, *We are all lesbians*" (*Search* 289).

The most androgynous character in *The Color Purple* is Shug Avery. She is the mother of three children, she is Albert's lover and long-time friend, and she becomes Celie's lover and companion. She is truly a womanist who is not afraid to live her life to the fullest. Shug inspires both Celie and "Mr. _____" to love, to express themselves in creative ways, and to become more androgynous. Celie and "Mr._____" conclude that Shug is not like men or women, that she is just different (*Color* 276). "In short, Shug and Celie, with a slight twist to the Pygmalion myth, personify that unifying principle and liberating experience exemplified by androgyny in all of Walker's novels" (Buncombe 426). While Jacobs and Hurston endow their protagonists with androgynous characteristics, Walker writes within the female dialogic by "destabilizing the terms masculine and feminine" and by creating at least one protagonist who is truly androgynous (Herrmann 19).

The narratives by Jacobs, Hurston, and Walker have a somewhat gendered relation of writer to reader. These three narratives were written, ultimately, to an audience that would read

as women. That is not to say that men could not, and should
not, read and identify with the protagonists of the narratives.
Jacobs makes it clear to whom she is writing, for she addresses
her narrative to the (white) women of the North. Hurston and
Walker do not specifically address their narratives, but it is
reasonable to conclude that their envisioned readers would
read as women. According to Sandra Kemp, "If 'masculine'
narration involves mastery over the world of things, the scene
of the feminine elicits the female reader, or the reader, male
or female, as a woman" (104). The female reader is initially
elicited in each of these narratives, for the universe is perceived by the women of these narratives, the reader is asked to
identify with a female, or in the case of Walker, a "womanist,"
point of view. While this point of view is also specifically African American, the gendered struggles of the protagonists, to
some extent, open the narrative perception to that of all women
and move that perception toward androgyny. According to
Barbara Christian, "women of color can no longer be perceived
as marginal to the empowerment of all American women and
that an understanding of their reality and imagination is essential to the process of change that the entire society must
undergo in order to transform itself" (*Black Feminist* 185). While
Jacobs speaks specifically to Northern white women, and
Hurston speaks to a more limited group of possibly African
American women, Walker closes the circle by not only making
her perspective applicable to all women, but offering a truly
androgynous transformation process that would benefit all
humans.

Works Cited

Primary Sources

Christian, Barbara. Personal interview. 4 April 1990.

Douglass, Frederick. *Narrative of the Life of Frederick Douglass, An American Slave: Written By Himself.* 1845. New York: Signet Classics, 1968.

———. *My Bondage and My Freedom.* 1855. Introd. Eric Foner. New York: Dover Publications, 1969, 464pp.

Hurston, Zora Neale. *Dust Tracks on a Road.* 1942. Foreword Maya Angelou. Afterword Henry Louis Gates, Jr. New York: Harper Perennnial, 1991, 278pp.

———. "How It Feels to Be Colored Me." *I Love Myself When I Am Laughing...And Then Again When I Am Looking Mean and Impressive: A Zora Neale Hurston Reader.* Ed. Alice Walker. Introd. Mary Helen Washington. New York: The Feminist Press, 1979. 152-164.

———. *Mules and Men.* 1935. Foreword Arnold Rampersad. Harper & Row, 1990, 309pp.

———. *Their Eyes Were Watching God.* 1937. Foreword Mary Helen Washington. Afterword Henry Louis Gates, Jr. New York: Harper & Row, 1990, 205pp.

Jacobs, Harriet A. *Incidents in the Life of a Slave Girl: Written by Herself.* 1861. Ed. and Introd. Jean Fagan Yellin. Cambridge: Harvard University Press, 1987, 306pp.

Walker, Alice. *The Color Purple.* 1982. New York: Pocket Books, 1985, 295pp.

———. *In Love and Trouble.* 1967. New York: Harcourt Brace Jovanovich, 1973, 138pp.

———. *In Search of Our Mother's Gardens: Womanist Prose.* New York: Harcourt Brace Jovanovich, 1983, 397pp.

———. Interview. *Black Women Writers at Work.* Ed. Claudia Tate. New York: Continuum: New York, 1983. 175-187.

————. *Living By The Word*. New York: Harcourt Brace Jovanovich, 1988.

————. *Meridian*. 1976. New York: Pocket Books, 1986, 220pp.

————. *Revolutionary Petunias and Other Poems*. 1971. New York: Harcourt Brace Jovanovich, 1973, 70pp.

————. *The Temple of My Familiar*. New York: Harcourt Brace Jovanovich, 1989, 416pp.

————. *The Third Life of Grange Copeland*. 1970. New York: Pocket Books, 1988, 346pp.

————. *You Can't Keep a Good Woman Down*. 1971. New York: Harcourt Brace Jovanovich, 1981, 167pp.

————. *Possessing the Secret of Joy*. New York: Simon & Schuster, 1992.

————. *Warrior Marks*: *Female Genital Mutilation and the Sexual Blinding of Women*. London: Jonathan Cape, 1993.

Secondary Sources

Altman, Janet Gurkin. *Epistolarity*: *Approaches to a Form*. Columbus: Ohio State University Press, 1982.

Andrews, William L. "The Novelization of Voice in Early African American Narrative," *PMLA* 105.1 (1990) 23-34.

————. *To Tell a Free Story*: *The First Century of Afro-American Autobiography, 1760-1865*. Chicago: University of Illinois Press, 1986.

Angelou, Maya. Foreword. *Dust Tracks on a Road*. 1942. By Zora Neale Hurston. Afterword. Henry Louis Gates, Jr. New York: Harper Perennial, 1990.

Awkward, Michael. *Inspiriting Influences*: *Tradition, Revision, and Afro-American Women's Novels*. New York: Columbia University Press, 1989.

Barthes, Roland. *A Barthes Reader*. Ed. Susan Sontag. New York: Hill and Wang, 1983.

Belenky, Mary Field, Blythe M. Clinchy, Nancy R. Goldberger, and Jill M. Tarule. *Women's Ways of Knowing*: *The Development of Self, Voice, and Mind*. New York: Basic Books, Inc., 1986.

Bell, Roseann P., Bettye J. Parker, and Beverly Guy-Sheftall. *Sturdy Black Bridges*: *Visions of Black Women in Literature*. New York: Anchor Press/ Doubleday, 1979.

Berlant, Lauren. "Race, Gender, and Nation in *The Color Purple*." *Critical Inquiry* 14 (Summer 1988): 831-859.

Blassingame, John. *The Slave Community: Plantation Life in the Antebellum South*. New York: Oxford University Press, 1972.

"The Blighted One," *The Ladies' Garland* 3:3 (1840) 57-60.

"The Blighted One," [Concluded] *The Ladies' Garland* 3:4 (1840) 81-84.

Booth, Wayne C. *The Rhetoric of Fiction*. Chicago: University of Chicago Press, Second Edition, 1983.

———. *The Company We Keep: An Ethics of Fiction*. Berkeley: University of California Press, 1988.

Braxton, Joanne. "Afra-American Culture and the Contemporary Literary Renaissance." *Wild Women in the Whirlwind: Afra-American Culture and the Contemporary Literary Renaissance*. Ed. Joanne M. Braxton and Andree Nicola Mclaughlin. New Brunswick: Rutgers University Press, 1990. xxi-xxx.

———. "Ancestral Presence: The Outraged Mother Figure in Contemporary Afra-American Writing." *Wild Women in the Whirlwind: Afra-American Culture and the Contemporary Literary Renaissance*. Ed. Joanne M. Braxton and Andree Nicola Mclaughlin. New Brunswick: Rutgers University Press, 1990. 299-315.

———. *Black Women Writing Autobiography: A Tradition Within a Tradition*. Philadelphia: Temple University Press, 1961.

Bröck, Sabine, and Anne Koenen. "Alice Walker in Search of Zora Neale Hurston: Rediscovering a Black Female Literary Tradition." *History and Tradition in Afro-American Culture*. Ed. Günter H. Lenz. Frankfurt/New York: Campus Verlag, 1984.

Buncombe, Marie H. "Androgyny As Metaphor in Alice Walker's Novels." *College Language Association Journal*. 30 (1987): 419-427.

Butterfield, Stephen. *Black Autobiography in America*. Amherst: University of Massachusetts Press, 1974.

Byerman, Keith E. *Fingering the Jagged Grain: Tradition and Form in Recent Black Fiction*. Athens, Ga.: The University of Georgia Press, 1985.

C.F.D. "Female Irreligion," *The Ladies' Companion*, July 1840, 111-113.

Callahan, John F. *In the African-American Grain: The Pursuit of Voice in Twentieth-Century Black Fiction*. Chicago: University of Illinois Press, 1988.

Carby, Hazel V. *Reconstructing Womanhood: The Emergence of the Afro-American Woman Novelist*. New York: Oxford University Press, 1987.

Chodorow, Nancy. *The Reproduction of Mothering: Psychoanalysis and the Sociology of Gender*. Berkeley, Calif.: University of California Press, 1978.

Christian, Barbara. *Black Feminist Criticism*: *Perspectives on Black Women Writers*. New York: Pergamon Press, 1985.

———. *Black Women Novelists*: *The Development of a Tradition, 1892-1976*. Westport, Conn.: Greenwood Press, 1980.

Cohn, Dorrit. *Transparent Minds*: *Narrative Modes for Presenting Consciousness in Fiction*. Princeton: Princeton University Press, 1987.

Culler, Jonathan. *Structuralist Poetics*: *Structuralism, Linguistics, and the Study of Literature*. Ithaca: Cornell, University Press, 1975.

Dasenbrock, Reed Way. *Imitating the Italians*: *Wyatt, Spenser, Synge, Pound, Joyce*. Baltimore: Md.: Johns Hopkins University Press, 1991.

Davis, Angela. "Reflections on the Black Woman's Role in the Community of Slaves," *Black Women in United States History*. Ed. Darlene Clark Hine. New York: Carlson Publishing Inc., 1990, 287-301.

de Beauvoir, Simone. *The Second Sex*. Trans. H. M. Parshley. New York: Knopf, 1953.

Dixon, Melvin. *Ride Out the Wilderness*: *Geography and Identity in Afro-American Literature*. Chicago: University of Chicago Press, 1987.

DuBois, W.E.B. *The Souls of Black Folk*. Intro. John Edgar Wideman. New York: Vintage Books, 1990.

Dworkin, Andrea. *Pornography*: *Men Possessing Women*. New York: Perigee Books, 1981.

Fishburn, Katherine. *Women in Popular Culture*: *A Reference Guide*. Westport, Conn.: Greenwood Press, 1982.

Fleischman, Suzanne. *Tense and Narrativity*: *From Medieval Performance to Modern Fiction*. Austin: University of Texas Press, 1990.

Flynn, Elizabeth A. "Composing as a Woman," *College Composition and Communication*. 39.4 (1988): 423-435.

Fogel, Robert William, and Engerman, Stanley L. *Time on the Cross*: *The Economics of American Negro Slavery*. Boston: Little, Brown & Company, 1974.

Fox-Genovese, Elizabeth. *Feminism Without Illusions*: *A Critique of Individualism*. Chapel Hill: The University of North Carolina Press, 1991.

———. "My Statue, My Self: Autobiographical Writings of Afro-American Women." *The Private Self*: *Theory and Practice of Women's Autobiographical Writings*. Ed. Shari Benstock. Chapel Hill: The University of North Carolina Press, 1988.

———. "Strategies and Forms of Resistance: Focus on Slave Women in the United States," *In Resistance*: *Studies in African, Afro-Caribbean and Afro-*

American History. Ed. Gary Y. Okihiro. Amherst: University of Massachusetts Press, 1986.

————. *Within the Plantation Household: Black and White Women of the Old South*. Chapel Hill: The University of North Carolina Press, 1988.

Friedman, Norman. "Point of View in Fiction: The Development of a Critical Concept." *PMLA* 70.5 (1955): 1160-1184.

Freud, Sigmund. *Civilization and Its Discontents*. Trans. Ed. James Strachey. New York: W.W. Norton & Co., 1961.

Froula, Christine. "The Daughter's Seduction: Sexual Violence in Literary History," *Signs: Journal of Women in Culture and Society*. 11.4 (1986) 621-642.

Gates, Jr., Henry Louis. *The Signifying Monkey: A Theory of African-American Literary Criticism*. New York: Oxford University Press, 1988.

Genette, Gerard. *Narrative Discourse: An Essay in Method*. Trans. Jane E. Lewin. Ithaca: Cornell University Press, 1980.

Genovese, Eugene D. *Roll, Jordan, Roll: The World the Slaves Made*. New York: Random House, 1972.

Gilbert, Sandra and Susan Gubar. *The Madwoman in the Attic*. New Haven: Yale University Press, 1979.

Gilligan, Carol. *In a Different Voice: Psychological Theory and Women's Development*. Cambridge, Mass., Harvard University Press, 1982.

Gwin, Minrose C. *Black and White Women of the Old South: The Peculiar Sisterhood in American Literature*. Knoxville: The University of Tennessee Press, 1985.

H.G. "Christianity and Woman," *The Ladies' Repository and Gatherings of the West: A Monthly Periodical Devoted to Literature and Religion* 3 (1843): 7-8.

Hemenway, Robert E. *Zora Neale Hurston: A Literary Biography*. Chicago: University of Chicago Press, 1977.

Herrmann, Anne. *The Dialogic and Difference: "An/Other Woman" in Virginia Woolf and Christa Wolf*. New York: Columbia University Press, 1989.

Hite, Molly. "Romance, Marginality, Matrilineage: Alice Walker's *The Color Purple* and Zora Neale Hurston's *Their Eyes Were Watching God*," *Novel* (1989): 257-273.

Hogue, W. Lawrence. *Discourse and the Other: The Production of the Afro-American Text*. Durham: Duke University Press, 1986.

Holloway, Karla F. C. *The Character of the Word: The Texts of Zora Neale Hurston*. New York: Greenwood Press, 1987.

Holt, Elvin. "Zora Neale Hurston and the Politics of Race: A Study of Selected Nonfictional Works." Diss. U of Kentucky, 1983.

hooks, bell. *Feminist Theory: From Margin to Center*. Boston: South End Press, 1984.

———. "Zora Neale Hurston: A Subversive Reading," *Matutu*. 3.6 (1989): 3-23.

Hugo, Richard. *The Triggering Town: Lectures and Essays on Poetry and Writing*. New York: W.W. Norton & Co., 1979.

Humm, Maggie. *Feminist Criticism: Women as Contemporary Critics*. New York: St. Martin's Press, 1986. "The Influence of Woman: Past and Present," *The Ladies' Companion* 13 September 1840: 245.

Iser, Wolfgang. "The Reading Process: A Phenomenological Approach." *Reader-Response Criticism: From Formalism to Post-Structuralism*. Ed. Jane P. Tompkins. Baltimore: Johns Hopkins University Press, 1987.

Jaynes, Gerald, Ed. *The Slave's Narrative*. New York: Oxford University Press, 1985.

Jaggar, Allison M. "Love and Knowledge: Emotion in Feminist Epistemology." *Gender/Body/Knowledge: Feminist Reconstructions of Being and Knowing*. Ed. Alison M. Jaggar and Susan R. Bordo. New Brunswick: Rutgers University Press, 1989.

Jakobson, Roman. *On Language*. Ed. Linda R. Waugh and Monique Monville-Burston. Cambridge: Harvard University Press, 1990.

Johnson, Barbara. "Thresholds of Difference: Structures of Address in Zora Neale Hurston," *Critical Inquiry*.12(Autumn 1985): 278-289.

Jordan, Jennifer. "Feminist Fantasies: Zora Neale Hurston's *Their Eyes Were Watching God*," *Tulsa Studies in Women's Literature*. 7(1988): 105-117.

Kalb, John D. "The Anthropological Narrator of Hurston's *Their Eyes Were Watching God, Studies in American Fiction* 16.2 (1988): 169-180.

Kappeler, Susanne. *The Pornography of Representation*.Minneapolis: University of Minnesota Press, 1986.

Karcher, Carolyn L. *The First Woman in the Republic: A Cultural Biography of Lydia Maria Child*. Durham, North Carolina: Duke University Press, 1994.

Kaufman, Linda S. *Discourses of Desire: Gender, Genre, and Epistolary Fiction*. Ithaca: Cornell University Press, 1986.

Keller, Catherine. *From a Broken Web: Separation, Sexism, and Self*. Boston: Beacon Press, 1986.

Kemp, Sandra. "'But how describe a world seen without a self?' Feminism, Fiction, and Modernism," *Critical Quarterly* 32.1 (1989): 99-115.

Kitch, Sally L. "Gender and Language: Dialect, Silence, and the Disruption of Discourse," *Women's Studies* 14 (1987): 65-78.

Krasner, James. "The Life of Women: Zora Neale Hurston and Female Autobiography." *Black American Literature Forum.* 23.1 (1989): 113-126.

Lanser, Susan Sniader. *The Narrative Act: Point of View in Prose Fiction.* Princeton: Princeton University Press, 1981.

———. "Toward a Feminist Narratology." *Style* 20.3 (1986): 341-363.

Marks, Elaine and Isabelle de Courtivron. *New French Feminisms: An Anthology.* New York: Schocken Books, 1981.

McCredie, Wendy. "Authority and Authorization in *Their Eyes Were Watching God*," *Black American Literary Forum* 16 (1982): 25-28.

McDowell, Deborah E. "The Changing Same: Generational Connections and Black Women Novelists." *Reading Black, Reading Feminist: A Critical Anthology.* Ed. Henry Louis Gates, Jr. New York: Meridian, 1990, 91-111.

———. "New Directions for Black Feminist Criticism." *The New Feminist Criticism: Essays on Women, Literature, and Theory.* Ed. Elaine Showalter. New York: Pantheon Books, 1985.

McFeely, William S. *Frederick Douglass.* New York: W.W. Norton & Co., 1991.

Maltz, Daniel N. and Ruth A. Borker. "A Cultural Approach to Male-Female Miscommunication." *Language and Social Identity.* Ed. John J. Gumperz. New York: Cambridge UP, 1982.

Miller, Jean Baker. *Toward a New Psychology of Women.* Boston: Beacon Press, 1976.

Mills, Sara, Lynne Pearce, Sue Spaull, and Elaine Millard. *Feminist Readings/Feminists Reading.* Charlottesville: U P of Virginia, 1989.

Moi, Toril. *Sexual/Textual Politics: Feminist Literary Theory.* New York: Methuen, 1985.

Niemtzow, Annette. "The Problematic of Self in Autobiography: The Example of the Slave Narrative." *The Art of Slave Narrative: Original Essays in Criticism and Theory.* Ed. John Sekora and Darwin T. Turner.Macomb, Ill.: Western Illinois University Press, 1982, 96-109.

O'Flaherty, Wendy Doniger. *Dreams, Illusions, and Other Realities.* Chicago: University of Chicago Press, 1984.

———. *Other People's Myths: The Cave of Echoes.* New York: Macmillan, 1988.

Ovid. *The Metamorphoses of Ovid*. Trans. and Introd. Mary M. Innes. New York: Penguin Books, 1955.

Parker-Smith, Bettye J. "Alice Walker's Women: In Search of Some Peace of Mind." *Black Women Writers (1950-1980): A Critical Evaluation*. Ed. Mari Evans. New York: Anchor Press/Doubleday, 1984, 479-495.

Perkins, Linda M. "The Impact of the 'Cult of True Womanhood' on the Education of Black Women," *Journal of Social Issues* 39 (1983) 17-28.

Pondrom, Cyrena N. "The Role of Myth in Hurston's *Their Eyes Were Watching God*," *American Literature* 58.2 (1986): 181-203.

Pratt, Mary Louise. *Toward a Speech Act Theory of Literary Discourse*. Bloomington: Indiana University Press, 1977.

Prince, Gerald. "Introduction to the Study of the Narratee," *Reader-Response Criticism: From Formalism to Post-Structuralism*. Ed. Jane Tompkins. Baltimore: Johns Hopkins University Press, 1987.

Prince, Gerald. *Narratology: The Form and Function of Narrative*. New York: Mouton Publishers, 1982.

Raynaud, Claudine. "Autobiography as a 'Lying' Session: Zora Neale Hurston's *Dust Tracks on a Road*." *Black Feminist Criticism and Critical Theory*. Ed. Joe Weixlmann and Houston A. Baker, Jr. Studies in Black American Literature III. Greenwood, Fla.: Penkevill Publishing Co., 1988.

Rich, Adrienne. *On Lies, Secrets, and Silence: Selected Prose, 1966-1978*. New York: W. W. Norton Inc., 1979.

Roberts, Diane. *The Myth of Aunt Jemima: Representations of Race and Region*. New York: Routledge, 1994.

Sadoff, Dianne F. "Black Matrilineage: The Case of Alice Walker and Zora Neale Hurston." *Signs: Journal of Women in Culture and Society*. 2.2 (1985): 4-26.

Schmidt, Rita Terezinha. "With My Sword in My Hand: The Politics of Race and Sex in the Fiction of Zora Neale Hurston." Diss. U of Pittsburgh, 1983.

Scholes, Robert. *Structuralism in Literature: An Introduction*. New Haven: Yale University Press, 1974.

Smith, Sidonie. *A Poetics of Women's Autobiography: Marginality and the Fictions of Self-Representation*. Bloomington: Indiana University Press, 1987.

Smith, Valerie. *Self-Discovery and Authority in Afro-American Narrative*. Cambridge: Harvard University Press, 1987.

Smith-Rosenberg, Carroll. *Disorderly Conduct: Visions of Gender in Victorian America*. New York: Alfred A. Knopf, 1985.

Southerland, Ellease. "The Influence of Voodoo on the Fiction of Zora Neale Hurston." *Sturdy Black Bridges: Visions of Black Women in Literature.* Eds. Roseann P. Bell, Bettye J. Parker, and Beverly Guy-Sheftall, New York: Anchor Press/Doubleday, 1979.

Spender, Dale. *Man Made Language.* London: Routledge & Kegan Paul, 1980.

Spillers, Hortense J. "Cross-Currents, Discontinuities: Black Women's Fiction." Afterword. *Conjuring: Black Women, Fiction, and Literary Tradition.* Eds. Marjorie Pryse and Hortense J. Spillers. Bloomington: Indiana University Press, 1984. 249-259.

St. Andrews, Bonnie. *Forbidden Fruit: On the Relationship Between Women and Knowledge in Doris Lessing, Selma Lagerlof, Kate Chopin, Margaret Atwood.* Troy, New York: Whitston Publishing, 1986.

Stepto, Robert B. *From Behind the Veil: A Study of Afro-American Narrative.* Chicago: University of Illinois Press, 1979.

Stuckey, Sterling. *The Slave Culture: Nationalist Theory and the Foundations of Black America.* New York: Oxford University Press, 1987.

Tate, Claudia. "Pauline Hopkins: Our Literary Foremother," *Conjuring: Black Women, Fiction, and Literary Tradition.* Ed. Marjorie Pryse and Hortense J. Spillers, Bloomington: Indiana University Press, 1984.

Tannen, Deborah. *You Just Don't Understand: Women and Men in Conversation.* New York: Ballantine Books, 1990.

Todorov, Tzvetan. *Introduction to Poetics.* Trans. Richard Howard. Minneapolis: University of Minnesota Press, 1981.

Wagner, Geoffrey. *Five for Freedom: A Study of Feminism in Fiction.* Rutherford, N.J.: Fairleigh Dickinson University Press, 1973.

Warhol, Robyn R. *Gendered Interventions: Narrative Discourse in the Victorian Novel.* New Brunswick: Rutgers University Press, 1989.

Washington, Mary Helen. "An Essay on Alice Walker." *Sturdy Black Bridges: Visions of Black Women in Literature.* Ed. Roseann P. Bell, Bettye J. Parker, and Beverly Guy-Sheftall. New York: Anchor Press/Doubleday, 1979.

———. Foreword. *Their Eyes Were Watching God.* By Zora Neal Hurston. Ed. Henry Louis Gates, Jr. New York: Harper & Row, 1990.

———. "'The Darkened Eye Restored': Notes Toward a Literary History of Black Women." *Reading Black, Reading Feminist: A Critical Anthology.* Ed. Henry Louis Gates, Jr. New York: Meridian, 1990. 30-43.

———. "Zora Neale Hurston: A Woman Half in Shadow," Introduction. *I Love Myself When I Am Laughing . . . And Then Again When I Am Looking Mean and Impressive: A Zora Neale Hurston Reader.* Ed. Alice Walker. New York: The Feminist Press, 1979. 7-25.

Welter, Barbara. "The Cult of True Womanhood: 1820-1860." *Our American Sisters: Women in American Life and Thought.*Eds. Jean E. Friedman and William G. Shade. Boston: Allyn and Bacon, Inc., 1973.

White, Deborah Gray. *Ar'n't I a Woman?* New York: W.W. Norton & Co., 1985.

"Woman's Sceptre," *Godey's Lady's Book and Magazine* 63 (July-December 1861): 305.

Woodward, C. Vann, Ed. *Mary Chesnut's Civil War*. New Haven: Yale University Press, 1981.

Woolf, Maria Tai. "Listening and Living: Reading and Experience in *Their Eyes Were Watching God*," *Black American Literary Forum* 16 (Spring 1982): 29-33.

Woolf, Virginia. *A Room of One's Own*. New York: Harcourt Brace Jovanovich, 1957.

Yellin, Jean Fagan. Introduction. *Incidents in the Life of a Slave Girl*. By Harriet A. Jacobs. Cambridge, Mass.: Harvard University Press, 1987.

————. *Women and Sisters: The Antislavery Feminists in American Culture*. New Haven: Yale University Press, 1989.

Notes

Introduction

1   See Barbara Christian, *Black Feminist Criticism*: *Perspectives on Black Women Writers* (New York: Pergamon Press, 1985). See also Henry Louis Gates, Jr., *The Signifying Monkey*: *À Theory of African-American Literary Criticism* (New York: Oxford University Press, 1988), and Michael Awkward, *Inspiriting Influences*: *Tradition, Revision, and Afro-American Women's Novels* (New York: Columbia University Press, 1989).

2   Michael McGuire argues that the potential of narrative to influence social-political attitudes is at "the heart of a rhetoric of narrtive". He defines rhetoric as "a theory of language that explains its potential to inform and persuade." See Michael McGuire, "The Rhetoric of Narrative: A Hermeneutic, Critical Theory," *Narrative Thought and Narrative Language*, ed. Bruce K. Britton and Anthony D. Pellegrini (Hillsdale, New Jersey, Lawrence Erlbaum Associates, Publishers, 1990): 219.

3   Reed Way Dasenbrock suggests that Bloom moves beyond the notion of individual precursors by indicating that "his system is less a matter of poets responding to other poets than of poems responding somehow to other poems." In his examination of the "intertextual" resemblance between works of English and Italian literature, Dasenbrock argues that writers consciously and intentionally imitate the works of others, that "literature is made up of works, not texts, created by individual authors working at specific (if not always specifiable) moments in history." See Reed Way Dasenbrock, *Imitating the Italians*: *Wyatt, Spenser, Synge, Pound, Joyce* (Baltimore: The Johns Hopkins University Press, 1991) 11. According to Henry Louis Gates, Jr., who specifically addresses the African American literary tradition, "by 1941 it was apparent . . . that black writers read, repeated, imitated, and revised each other's texts to a remarkable extent." See Henry Louis Gates, Jr., *The Signifying Monkey*: *A Theory of African-American Literary Criticism* (New York: Oxford University Press, 1988) xxii.

4   Wayne Booth states: "the author creates, in short, an image of himself and another image of his reader; he makes his reader, as he makes his second self, and the most successful reading is one in which the created selves, author and reader, can find complete agreement." See

Wayne Booth, *The Rhetoric of Fiction* (Chicago: University of Chicago Press, 1961) 138.

5   Mary Louise Pratt states: "In sum, speech act theory provides a way of talking about utterances not only in terms of their surface grammatical properties but also in terms of the context in which they are made, the intentions, attitudes, and expectations of the participants, the relationships existing between participants, and generally, the unspoken rules and conventions that are understood to be in play when an utterance is made and received." Cited in Mary Louise Pratt, *Toward a Speech Act Theory of Discourse* (Bloomington: Indiana University Press, 1977) 86.

6   See Mary Field Belenky, Blythe M. Clinchy, Nancy R. Goldberger, and Jill M. Tarule, *Women's Ways of Knowing: The Development of Self, Voice, and Mind* (New York: Basic Books, Inc., 1986).

7   Joanne M. Braxton discusses the unwritten African American tradition that gave rise to the written tradition of the nineteenth century. Writers such as Lucy Terry, Phillis Wheatley, Harriet E. Wilson, Harriet A. Jacobs, Frances Ellen Watkins Harper contributed to the twentieth century authorship of Zora Neale Hurston, Jessie Fauset, and Nella Larsen. See Joanne Braxton, *Wild Women in the Whirlwind: A Tradition Within a Tradition* (Philadelphia: Temple University Press, 1961) xxii. Claudia Tate lists "foremothers" who, like Hurston, present protagonists who have no early knowledge of their African heritage. She includes Frances Harper in the list. See Claudia Tate, " Pauline Hopkins: Our Literary Foremother," *Conjuring: Black Women, Fiction, and Literary Tradition*, ed. Marjorie Pryse and Hortense J. Spillers (Bloomington: Indiana University Press, 1985) 53-66.

8   Genette argues that the narrator has already become someone else after the event, and that the letter really reflects this "point of view." See Gerard Genette, *Narrative Discourse: An Essay in Method*, trans. Jane E. Lewin (New York: Cornell University Press, 1980) 217-218.

9   As cited in Christine Froula, "The Daughter's Seduction: Sexual Violence and Literary History," *Signs: Journal of Women in Culture and Society* 11.4 (1986): 422.

Chapter One

1   Pratt elaborates: "What a speaker implicates on a given occasion is distinguishable from what he says, that is from the literal and conventional meaning of the words he uses; what is said and what is implicated together form the meaning of the utterance in that context." See Mary Louise Pratt, *Toward a Speech Act Theory of Discourse* (Bloomington: Indiana University Press, 1977) 154.

2   William L. Andrews describes Lydia Maria Child's traditional identification with literary sentimentalism and its effect on Jacobs's writing. See William L. Andrews, *To Tell a Free Story: The First Century of Afro-American Autobiography, 1760-1865* (Chicago: University of Illinois Press, 1986). Annette Niemtzow, while recognizing that Jacobs had no choice but to use the form of the domestic or what she terms "seduction" novel, believes that the form caused her ultimately to fail in her quest for self and voice. See Annette Niemtzow, "The Problematic of Self in Autobiography: The Example of the Slave Narrative," *The Art of Slave Narrative: Original Essays in Criticism and Theory*, ed. John Sekora and Darwin R. Turner (Macomb, Ill.: Western Illinois University, 1982) 97-109.

3   Carolyn L. Karcher examines Child's careful editing of the volume. Child suggested the order of the book, the ending, and gathered the "savage cruelties" that women endured into one chapter of the book, so that readers whose sensibilities would be offended might omit this chapter. See Carolyn L. Karcher, *The First Woman in the Republic: A Cultural Biography of Lydia Maria Child*, Durham, North Carolina: Duke University Press, 1994.

4   According to Gerald Prince, "The portrait of a narratee emerges above all from the narrative addressed to him." This portrait can be constructed from signals sent by the narrator, signals that include direct address, second-person pronouns, and verb forms. See Gerald Prince, "Introduction to the Study of the Narratee," *Reader-Response Criticism: From Formalism to Post-Structuralism*, ed. Jane Tompkins, (Baltimore: Johns Hopkins University Press, 1987) 12-25.

5   Jacobs's need to overjustify her situation is a result of the double-bind of race and sex. According to Sidonie Smith, the script for women's lives is a product of the patriarchal culture; thus, the "woman of color" was a doubly marginalized figure, "always removed from the center of power within the culture she inhabits. Moreover, her nonpresence, her unrepresentability, presses even more imperiously yet elusively on her; and her position as speaker before an audience becomes even more precarious." See Sidonie Smith, *A Poetics of Women's Autobiography: Marginality and the Fictions of Self-Representation* (Bloomington: Indiana University Press, 1987) 51.

6   Differences found in narrative gender strategies are certainly not the result of biological sex differences. It is worth noting that Douglass does not use distancing strategies in his second autobiography, *My Bondage and My Freedom*. In fact, he uses engaging tactics that are very similar to Jacobs's. He directly addresses his audience as "dear reader," "the reader," or "my kind reader," in at least eighteen instances. See Frederick Douglass, *My Bondage and My Freedom* (New York: Dover Publications, 1969).

7　　Mary Chesnut would certainly agree with Harriet Jacobs. Her diary
　　　entry for Mary 18, 1861 is a denunciation of miscegenation and a
　　　recognition of the denial practiced by southern white women. See C.
　　　Vann Woodward, ed., *Mary Chesnut's Civil War*. (New Haven: Yale Uni-
　　　versity Press, 1981), pp. 29, 31.

8　　William L. Andrews stresses, however, that dialogization of voice rep-
　　　resented a break with discursive conventions. It was this very innova-
　　　tion, or signification, that created the "long-standing doubts about
　　　the fictionality, that is, the untrustworthiness, of *Incidents*." See Will-
　　　iam L. Andrews, "The Novelization of Voice in Early African Ameri-
　　　can Narrative," *PMLA* 105.1 (1990) 23.

9　　According to Elizabeth Fox-Genovese, Harriet Jacobs, "structured her
　　　entire account of her escape from slavery as a remorseless and unme-
　　　diated struggle against the imposition of her master's will. Although
　　　the narrative includes much on her sexuality and her children, and
　　　her master's sexual designs upon her—so much as to have earned it a
　　　description as a modern *Pamela*—in the end everything falls by the
　　　wayside except her own refusal to accept the imposition of his will."
　　　See Elizabeth Fox-Genovese, "Strategies and Forms of Resistance: Focus
　　　on Slave Women in the United States," *In Resistance: Studies in Afri-
　　　can, Afro-Caribbean and Afro-American History*, ed. Gary Okihiro
　　　(Amherst: University of Massachusetts Press, 1986) 161.

10　　See Roman Jakobson, "The Speech Event and the Functions of Lan-
　　　guage," *On Language: Roman Jakobson*, ed. Linda R. Waugh and
　　　Monique Monville-Burston (Cambridge, Mass.: Harvard University
　　　Press, 1990).

11　　Elizabeth Fox-Genovese does not believe that Jacobs actually spent
　　　seven years in confinement: "If specific details such as the duration
　　　of her hiding, the size of her hiding space, and the letters from her
　　　master are altogether improbable, their very improbability serve as
　　　reminders that Jacobs's book should be read as a crafted representa-
　　　tion—as a fiction or a cautionary tale." *Within the Plantation House-
　　　hold: Black and White Women of the Old South* (Chapel Hill: University
　　　of North Carolina Press, 1991) 392. Fox-Genovese's article in Shari
　　　Benstock's *The Private Self* is more direct: "Jacobs's narrative embod-
　　　ies every conceivable element of fantasy and ambiguity." See Eliza-
　　　beth Fox-Genovese, "My Statue, My Self: Autobiographical Writings
　　　of Afro-American Women," *The Private Self: Theory and Practice of
　　　Women's Autobiographical Writings* (Chapel Hill: University of North
　　　Carolina Press, 1988) 76.

12　　According to Gerald Prince, there are many narratives with more than
　　　one narratee. "When there are two or more, the one to whom all of
　　　the events recounted are ultimately addressed is the main narratee.
　　　One the other hand, one who is told only some of the events is a

secondary narratee; and so on." See Gerald Prince, *Narratology: The Form and Functioning of Narrative* (New York: Mouton Publishers, 1982) 24.

13   Elizabeth Fox-Genovese states that it is unrealistic for the reader to believe that Jacobs eluded her master's sexual advances. In a note she relates a conversation with Bell Hooks. Hooks argues "that the silence at the center of the narrative veils Linda Brent's rape by her master." See Elizabeth Fox-Genovese, *Within the Plantation Household: Black and White Women of the Old South* (Chapel Hill: University of North Carolina Press, 1988) 462.

14   For a more complete discussion of this subject, See Wolfgang Iser, *The Implied Reader: Patterns of Communication in Prose Fiction from Bunyan to Becket* (Baltimore: Johns Hopkins University Press, 1974).

15   Diane Roberts states that Child's editing of *Incidents* was a method of "testing the boundaries of gender decorum and redefining chastity," a means of breaking the rigid boundaries of womanly purity and goodness. Roberts offers an excellent discussion of Child's proposal to end racial conflict in America through intermarriage or "almagamation" of the races. See Diane Roberts, *The Myth of Aunt Jemima: Representations of Race and Region.* (New York: Routledge, 1994), pp. 127-152.

16   Deborah Gray White considers Blassingame's work a "classic" byt notes that "much of it deals with male status" (21). See Deborah Gray White, *Ar'n't I a Woman?.* New York: W. W. Norton & Company, 1985.

17   For a more complete discussion of the work ethic of slaves, see Gerald Jaynes, "Plantations and the Slave Work Ethic," in *The Slave's Narrative*, Ed. Charles T. Davis and Henry Louis Gates, Jr. (New York, 1985) pp. 98-112. For somewhat opposing viewpoints of how the slaves viewed the work ethic, see also Robert W. Fogel and Stanley Engermann, *Time on the Cross: The Economics of American Slavery* (New York, 1972), and Eugene D. Genovese, *Roll Jordan Roll: The World the Slaves Made* (New York, 1972).

18   For an essay on Rebecca Jackson, see Alice Walker, "Gifts of Power: The Writings of Rebecca Jackson," *In Search of Our Mother's Gardens: Womanist Prose By Alice Walker* (New York: Harcourt Brace Jovanovich, 1983) 71-82.

19   There is some suspicion that Mr. Covey was homosexual, but that Douglass, like Jacobs, was unable to record the explicit details of the sexual coercion he faced. In commenting on the scene in which Mr. Covey rushed at Douglass, tore off his clothes, and lashed him with switches, William S. McFeely states: "This was as close as a Victorian author could come to speaking about the sadistic abuse of males by males. Covey's savage attack strongly suggests a perversion of homo-

sexual attraction into vicious cruelty." See William S. McFeely, *Frederick Douglass* (New York: W. W. Norton & Co., 1991) 44.

Chapter Two

1   Hurston's birthdate has been revised in recent years to 1891. There has been much speculation as to why she chose to conceal her real birthdate. See Arnold Rampersad, preface, *Their Eyes Were Watching God*, by Zora Neale Hurston (New York: Harper & Row, 1990) xix.

2   According to Mary Helen Washington, Mrs. Osgood Mason was "an extremely controlling woman" and Hurston "was kept walking a tight-rope so as not to offend her." Hurston did sign a contract with Mason that granted her an allowance of two hundred dollars per month to collect folklore in the South. It is estimated that Mason "gave Hurston approximately fifteen thousand dollars for her work and self-support" over a five year period. This money, however, was hardly sufficient for the travel and research necessary for Hurston's anthropological studies. See Mary Helen Washington, introduction, *I Love Myself When I Am Laughing . . . And Then Again When I Am Looking Mean and Impressive: A Zora Neale Hurston Reader*, by Zora Neale Hurston, ed. by Alice Walker, (New York: The Feminist Press, 1979) 12-13.

3   For a more complete descriptions of these transformations, see Ovid, *The Metamorphoses of Ovid*, trans. Mary M. Innes (New York: Penguin Books, 1955) 45, 63, 212.

4   Cyrena N. Pondrom less convincingly describes Tea Cake as the "mythic consort of an avatar of the great female goddess. One of the most important elements in this is Tea Cake's youth. The Ishtar-Tammuz, Aphrodite-Adonis, and Isis-Osiris myths are all tales of love between an older woman and a younger man." See Cyrena N. Pondrom, "The Role of Myth in Hurston's *Their Eyes Were Watching God*," *American Literature* 58.2 (1986): 192.

5   Cyrena N. Pondrom describes the narrator of *Their Eyes* as an "implied narrator" who "is a person of folk wisdom and rich black experience who is able to represent the minds and speech of Pheoby, Janie, Nanny, and 'old buzzard Parson' in turn, integrating all into a vision of experience that is finally mythic." see Cyrena N. Pondrom, "The Role of Myth in Hurston's *Their Eyes Were Watching God*," *American Literature* 58.2 (1986): 188.

6   See John D. Kalb, "The Anthropological Narrator of Hurston's *Their Eyes Were Watching God*," *Studies in American Fiction* (1989): 168-180. Also see Robert B. Stepto, *From Behind the Veil: A Study of Afro-American Narrative* (Chicago: U of Illinois P, 1979) 164-167.

7   According to Henry Louis Gates Jr., "There are well over two dozen repetitions of the figure of the tree in this text." Gates also discusses

the importance of the god Legba and his/her manifestations. See Henry Louis Gates Jr., *The Signifyin(g) Monkey* (New York: Oxford UP, 1988) 186. Ellease Southerland states that "the tree is the symbol of the god Legba, the god who provides a way. The tree is the connection between heaven and earth; it is a medium for spirits" Also see Ellease Southerland, "The Influence of Voodoo on the Fiction of Zora Neale Hurston," *Sturdy Black Bridges: Visions of Black Women in Literature*, ed. by Roseann P. Bell, Bettye J. Parker, and Beverly Guy-Sheftall, (New York: Anchor Press/Doubleday, 1979) 179.

8　See Susan S. Lanser, "Toward a Feminist Narratology," *Style* 20.3 (1986): 348-351.

9　Butterfield identifies the first phase of African American autobiography as the last two decades before the Civil War. In this period "the slave narratives came to full maturity and most of their authors were taking prominent roles in the antislavery crusade." The last phase of autobiography, after 1961, "shows a resurgence of political purpose and a trend toward more colloquial language." See Stephen Butterfield, *Black Autobiography in America* (Amherst: University of Massachusetts Press, 1974) 6-7.

Chapter Three

1　According to Hugo, "With the private poet, and most good poets of the last century or so have been private poets, the words, at least certain key words, mean something to the poet they don't mean to the reader." See Richard Hugo, *The Triggering Town: Lectures and Essays on Poetry and Writing* (New York: W.W. Norton & Co., 1985) 14.

2　See Andrea Dworkin, *Pornography: Men Possessing Women* (London, The Women's Press, 1981) 101-128. See also Elaine Marks and Isabelle Courtivron, Eds., *New French Feminisms* (New York, Schocken Books, 1981).

3　Walker defines a *womanist* as "A black feminist or feminist of color. From the black folk expression of mothers to female children, 'You acting womanish, i.e., like a woman. Usually referring to outrageous, audacious, courageous or *willful* behavior. Wanting to know more and in greater depth than is considered 'good' for one...*Also*: A woman who loves other women, sexually and/or nonsexually. Cited in Alice Walker, *In Search of Our Mother's Gardens* (New York: Harcourt Brace Jovanovich, 1983) xi.

4　While many African women writers, wuch as Flora Nwapa, prefer the African American term "womanist" to the tag "feminist," they have some reservations about embracing Walkerian womanism. The reservations relate to lesbianism. Nwapa is silent on the matter but other writers such as Bessie Head have noted the sentiments against homosexuality. See Chikweny Okonjo Ogunyemi, *African Wo/man Palava*: *The Nigerian Novel by Women*. Chicago: The Unversity of Chicago Press, 1995.

5   Keller took the term "oceanic feeling" from letters exchanged between Romain Rolland and Sigmund Freud. Rolland wrote a letter in response to Freud's *The Future of an Illusion*. Freud explains Rolland's use of the term: "It is a feeling which he would like to call a sensation of 'eternity', a feeling as of something limitless, unbounded—as it were 'oceanic'." Cited in Sigmund Freud, *Civilization and Its Discontents* Ed. James Strachey (New York: W. W. Norton & Co., 1961).

6   See also Linda S. Kaufman, *Discourses of Desire*: *Gender, Genre, and Epistolary Fiction* (Ithaca, Cornell University Press, 1986).

7   For a more complete discussion of African American music and oral tradition using the call-and-response method see John F. Callahan, *In the African-American Grain*: *The Pursuit of Voice in Twentieth-Century Black Fiction* (Chicago: Illinois University Press, 1988).

8   Keith Byerman considers *The Color Purple* a "womanist" fairy tale because Celie overcomes tragedy and travail, emerges as a "princess," and lives happily every after. Found in Keith Byerman, *Fingering the Jagged Grain: Tradition and Form in Recent Black Fiction* (Athens: Georgia University Press, 1985) 161.

9   The subject of Buchi Emecheta's novel, *The Family*, is also incest. According to Chikwenye Ogunyemi, "Emecheta revises such predecessor's works as Ralph Ellison's *Invisible Man*, James Baldwin's *Just Above My Head*, Toni Morrison's *The Bluest Eye*, Gayl Jones's *Corregidor* and Alice Walker's *The Color Purple*. With the continued erosion of black power in a racist universe and the consequent sociopolitical chaos, black women writers present incest as a ripple effect of black historical disengranchisement in the public domain. Incest manifests itself as the internalization of the despicable: a tragic inward turn through which the black man misuses his paltry power, expresses his rage by preying on his weak daughter, violates boundaries, and betrays her trust. Emecheta gives incest a face and a name. She insists that incest produces female victims who withstand the stresses of a vicious war" (271). See Ogunyemi, Chikwenye Okonjo. *Africa Wo/man Palava: The Negerian Novel by Women*.1995. Chicago: The University of Chicago Press. See also Emecheta, Buchi. *The Family*. 1990. New York: George Braziller.

10   I am referring to Nettie as a semi-public narrator because Celie is presenting her letters extant. Nettie is thus creating her own fictional world. See Susan S. Lanser, *The Narrative Act*: *Point of View in Prose Fiction*. (Princeton: Princeton University Press, 1981) 137.

Chapter Four

1 Bonnie St. Andrews discusses the history of the denial of knowledge to women in sacred tales and secular st ories. She also outlines the subsequent determination of women " for ethical self-rule" which she later refers to as "self-governance." See Bonnie St. Andrews, *Forbidden Fruit*: *On the Relationship Between Women and Knowledge* (New York: Whitston Publishing, 1986) x, 10.

2 Cited in Bonnie St. Andrews, *Forbidden Fruit*. St. Andrews took the term from a lecture Welty presented to the Mississippi Historical Society. Welty demonstrated how "ironic modification" was used and "discusses it uses in `Fairy Tale of the Natchez Trace,' her lecture." See Bonnie St. Andrews, *Forbidden Fruit*: *On the Relationship Between Women and Knowledge* (New York: Whitston Publishing, 1986) 12.

3 Unlike Janie or Celie, Edna Pontellier's "awakening" had disastrous results, for she was truly bound by the "cult of true womanhood." See Kate Chopin, *The Awakening & Selected Stories*, Intro. Nina Baym (New York: Random House Inc., 1981).

4 According to Mary Helen Washington, "One white review in 1937 praised the novel in the *Saturday Review* as a `rich and racy love story, if somewhat awkward,' but had difficulty believing that such a town as Eatonville, `inhabited and governed entirely by Negroes,' could be real. Black male critics were much harsher in their assessments of the novel. From the beginning of her career, Hurston was severely criticized for not writing fiction in the protest tradition." Cited in Zora Neale Hurston, *Their Eyes Were Watching God*. Foreword by Mary Helen Washington, (New York: Harper & Row, 1990) vii.

5 5The subject of confinement as protest by women is explored further by Gilbert and Gubar. See Sandra Gilbert and Susan Gubar, *The Madwoman in the Attic* (New Haven: Yale University Press, 1979).

6 For a more complete discussion of feminist discourse, see Josephine Donovan, ed., *Feminist Literary Criticism*: *Explorations in Theory*, 2nd ed. (Lexington: University Press of Kentucky, 1989).

7 Daniel N. Maltz and Ruth A. Borker list five characteristics of speech strategies used by women. Interruptions are one of these characteristics and are extremely common. Unlike the interruptions made by men, however, women interrupt discourse to call for "elaboration and development" and their interruptions are taken as "signs of support and interest." Daniel N. Maltz and Ruth A. Borker, "A Cultural Approach to Male-Female Miscommunication," *Language and Social Identity*, ed. John J. Gumperz (New York: Cambridge University Press, 1982) 210.

8   Some feminists are critical of the search for differences because they believe that it reinforces a rigid structuration of what is to be considered male and female. See Toril Moi, *Sexual/Textual Politics*: *Feminist Literary Theory* (New York: Methuen, 1985) 150-173. See also Julia Kristeva, *The Kristeva Reader*, ed. Toril Moi (New York: Columbia University Press, 1986).

Index

ADY-2338